REJECTED
SUNDAY SCHOOL LESSONS

STEVEN CASE

ZONDERVAN

ZONDERVAN.com/
AUTHORTRACKER
follow your favorite authors

youth specialties

youth specialties

Rejected Sunday School Lessons
Copyright © 2007 by Steven Case

Youth Specialties products, 300 S. Pierce St., El Cajon, CA 92020 are published by Zondervan, 5300 Patterson Ave. SE, Grand Rapids, MI 49530.

ISBN-10: 0-310-28042-7
ISBN-13: 978-0-310-28042-2

All Scripture quotations, unless otherwise indicated, are taken from the Holy Bible: New International Version®. NIV®. Copyright © 1973, 1978, 1984 by International Bible Society. Used by permission of Zondervan. All rights reserved.

All rights reserved. No part of this publication may be reproduced, stored in a retrieval system, or transmitted in any form or by any means — electronic, mechanical, photocopy, recording, or any other — except for brief quotations in printed reviews, without the prior permission of the publisher.

Web site addresses listed in this book were current at the time of publication. Please contact Youth Specialties via e-mail (YS@YouthSpecialties.com) to report URLs that are no longer operational and provide replacement URLs if available.

Interior design by David Conn

Printed in the United States of America

07 08 09 10 11 12 13 • 19 18 17 16 15 14 13 12 11 10 9 8 7 6 5 4 3 2 1

CONTENTS ~~REJECTED~~

INTRODUCTION 5

LESSON 1	GOT A MATCH?	9
LESSON 2	TROUBLE IN MIND	13
LESSON 3	POVERTY SUCKS	17
LESSON 4	GUESS WHICH HAND	21
LESSON 5	THE SUN WILL COME OUUUUUUUUT TOMORROW	25
LESSON 6	GOOOOOOAAAALLLLLLLLLLL!	29
LESSON 7	JESUS FOR DUMMIES	33
LESSON 8	HERE A BEAR, THERE A BEAR…	37
LESSON 9	ADAM TAKES A RIBBING	41
LESSON 10	HEAD, SHOULDERS, KNEES, AND TOES (KNEES AND TOES)…	45
LESSON 11	DANCE, YOU SON OF GOD, DANCE!	49
LESSON 12	PLOP PLOP, FIZZ FIZZ	53

REJECTED

SUNDAY SCHOOL LESSONS

LESSON 13	THE NEW KID IN TOWN	57
LESSON 14	IT'S MOVING DAY!	61
LESSON 15	PHARAOH PHAWCETT MAJORS	65
LESSON 16	SWIMMING FOR JESUS	69
LESSON 17	IN DEEP SHIP	73
LESSON 18	IT'S A BOY! (*OR* THE BIRTH OF THE CHURCH)	77
LESSON 19	NNNNNNEXT!	81
LESSON 20	THE HILLS ARE ALIIIIIIIIIVVVVVVVE	85
LESSON 21	PIMP MY RIDE	89
LESSON 22	CAN YOU HEAR ME *NOW?*	93
LESSON 23	GETTING IN OVER YOUR HEAD	97
LESSON 24	HE CAN FLY!	101

INTRODUCTION ~~REJECTED~~

Mrs. Mallot taught my kindergarten Sunday school class. She was a nice lady who wore lots of polyester and too much makeup. (I remember her eyebrows were one thin line that made her look as though she were really, really awake.) She also chewed gum all the time, and it made a loud cracking noise.

Mrs. Mallot was the first person to introduce me to the concept of the flannel board. She also showed me the first picture of God that I can remember. In the picture he wore a long, blue robe, and he sat on a heavenly throne while cherubim and seraphim fluttered about his head. He had white skin, long white hair, and a white beard. I also remember he didn't look very happy. Now, in my so-called adult mind, I remember it as being a look of "constipation."

"See? That's God," she said with a finality that cemented the image into my head for the rest of my life. I've had many conversations about the nature of God with many learned people. (Well, okay—with youth ministers whose opinions I respect.) *What is God? Who is God? What does God put on his toast?* That sort of thing. But no matter how many books I read, I still have that wonderful flannelgraph image of a constipated God stuck in my brain. He's there forever. Thank you, Mrs. Mallot.

The late great comedian W.C. Fields once said, "There isn't a man alive who hasn't wanted to boot a kid."

This book was born out of the artwork herein. French artist Gustave Doré (1832-1883) produced hundred of works like these in his lifetime. I was working as a director of Christian education when one of the Sunday school teachers asked me

REJECTED

SUNDAY SCHOOL LESSONS

for a picture of The Flood to use with her first-grade class. I did some searching and ran across the wonderful work that you see on page 68. I photocopied it and slid it into her lesson planner. Rumor has it she blew one of those icy things from Starbucks out her nose, but I wasn't there to see it.

Why would we create a book like this?

Three reasons—
1) Because God laughs, too. God is not a constipated, old, white man sitting on the throne of heaven and looking down on us with disapproval. God is love—and love and laughter are best friends.

2) Because a book like this is necessary to stay sane in this business. I'm told that Chuck Jones once produced a secret cartoon in which Wile E. Coyote actually caught and ate the Road Runner. The Disney animators regularly slip in little presents for sharp-eyed viewers who know how to use the freeze frame buttons on their remotes. I'm sure Charles Schulz once drew a picture of Charlie Brown punting Lucy's head over the goalpost. It's like a release button. Sometimes our faith can feel tight. Especially when others use the faith to straighten us out or rid us of untidy things. Sometimes working with God's children can resemble that rocket toy you fill with water and then slowly pump air into the chamber until you can't fit any more in. Along similar lines, this book can serve as a release button whenever you feel the work of youth ministry is getting a little tight.

3) Because at some point in time, every Sunday school teacher in the world has wanted to boot a kid.

—Steven Case

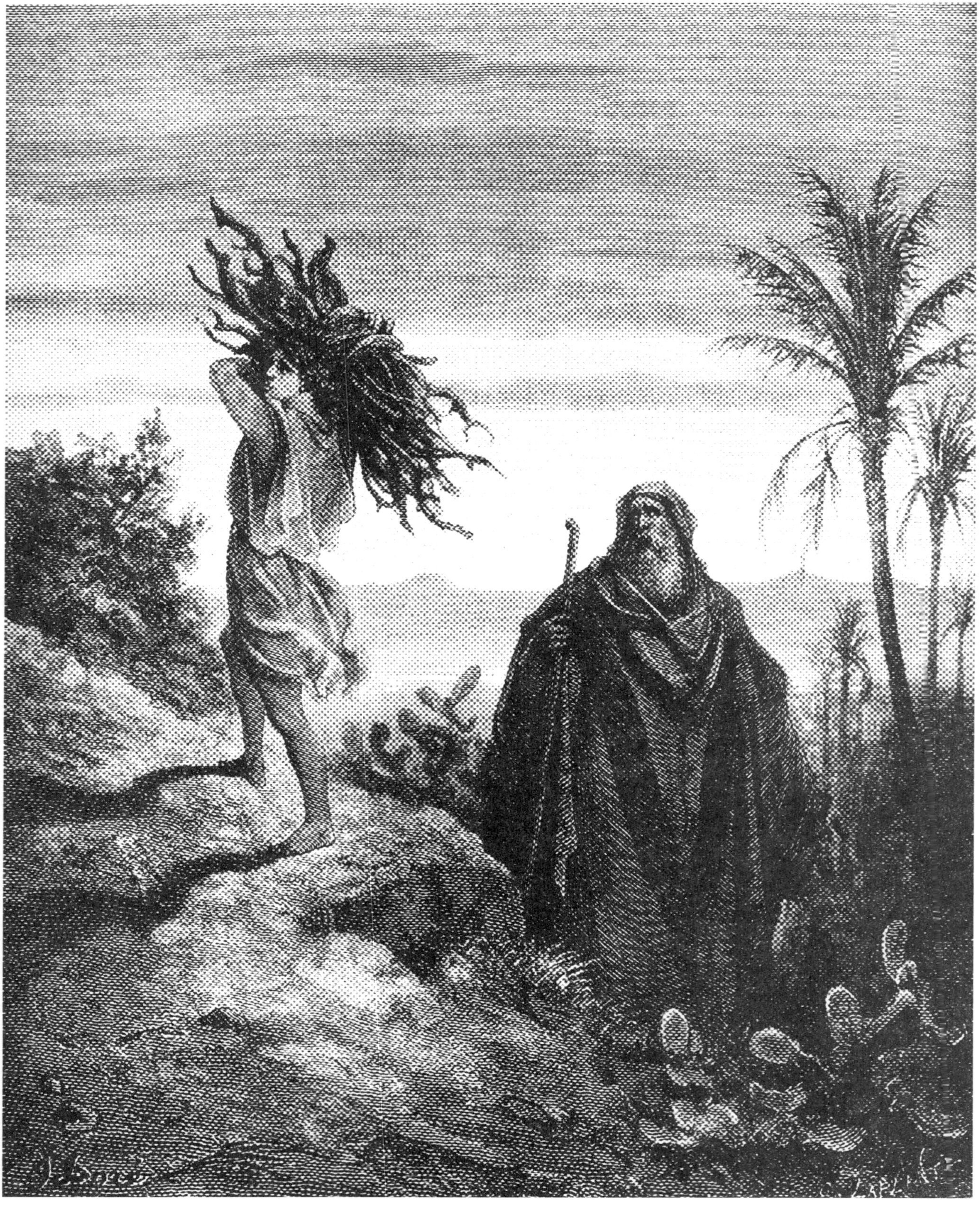

LESSON 1
GOT A MATCH?

REJECTED

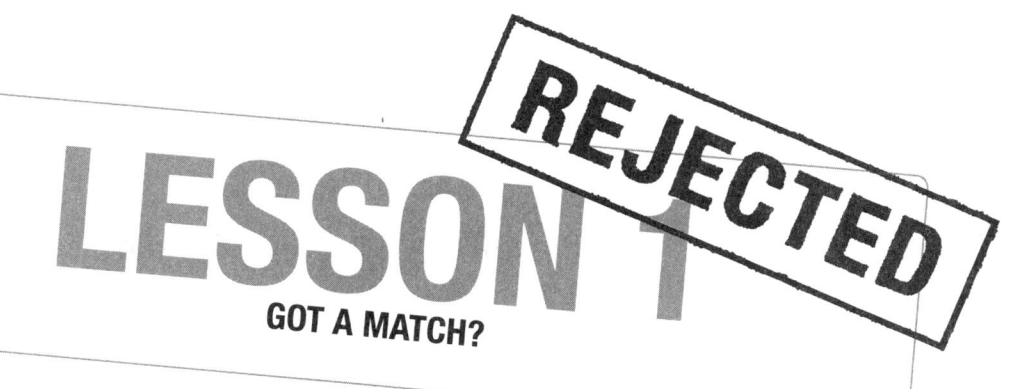

SCRIPTURE: Genesis 22:1-12
MAIN POINT: Obey your parents.

CHILDREN'S ACTIVITY

After reading the story of Abraham and Isaac, tell the children they're going to build an altar for a sacrifice. Have them look either inside the church building or on the church grounds for things they can burn. Of course you aren't *really* going to sacrifice anything (or anyone). You can just pretend to put a child on the altar or strap a paper lamb to the sticks. If you're holding this lesson outside, you can actually light a fire and have a hot dog roast or make s'mores for a snack.

DISCUSSION QUESTIONS

• Did God really want people to burn animals as part of their worship? (*Yes, God expected sacrifices.*)

• Why don't we do that anymore? (*Because Jesus said God was tired of the smell.*)

• Did Abraham ever tell Sarah that he was going to sacrifice Isaac? (*Probably not. Sometimes daddies have to keep secrets from mommies. Isaac's name means "laughter," so if Sarah did find out, Abraham probably told her he was only kidding.*)

• Isn't it kind of mean to ask a dad to sacrifice his own son? (*God wasn't really going to let Abraham kill Isaac. He just wanted to test Abraham.*)

• Would God ever ask our parents to do that? (*Probably not. But let's hope our mommies and daddies never have to find out.*)

TEACHER HELPS

• If any child asks, "What are we going to sacrifice?" look at them very intently and say, "God will provide."

REJECTED

- Show the children that Isaac was an obedient child. He built the altar because his father asked him to. Talk with the children about the importance of doing yard work and other chores around the house simply because Mommy or Daddy asks.

- Point out how in the picture it looks as though Abraham is standing near some cacti. Tell the children that even if Abraham stepped on a cactus while wearing his sandals, he wouldn't say any bad words. (*You might see some kids look a little worried at this point because of something they may have heard their mommies or daddies say. Tell them it's okay because God forgave their parents when Jesus died on the cross, so God will probably forgive their mommies and daddies for saying bad words, too.*)

- Point out that Isaac's parents were really, really old and would probably die soon; ask the children how old their parents are.

CLOSING PRAYER

God, thank you for not wanting burnt sacrifices anymore. We love our puppies the way they are. Amen.

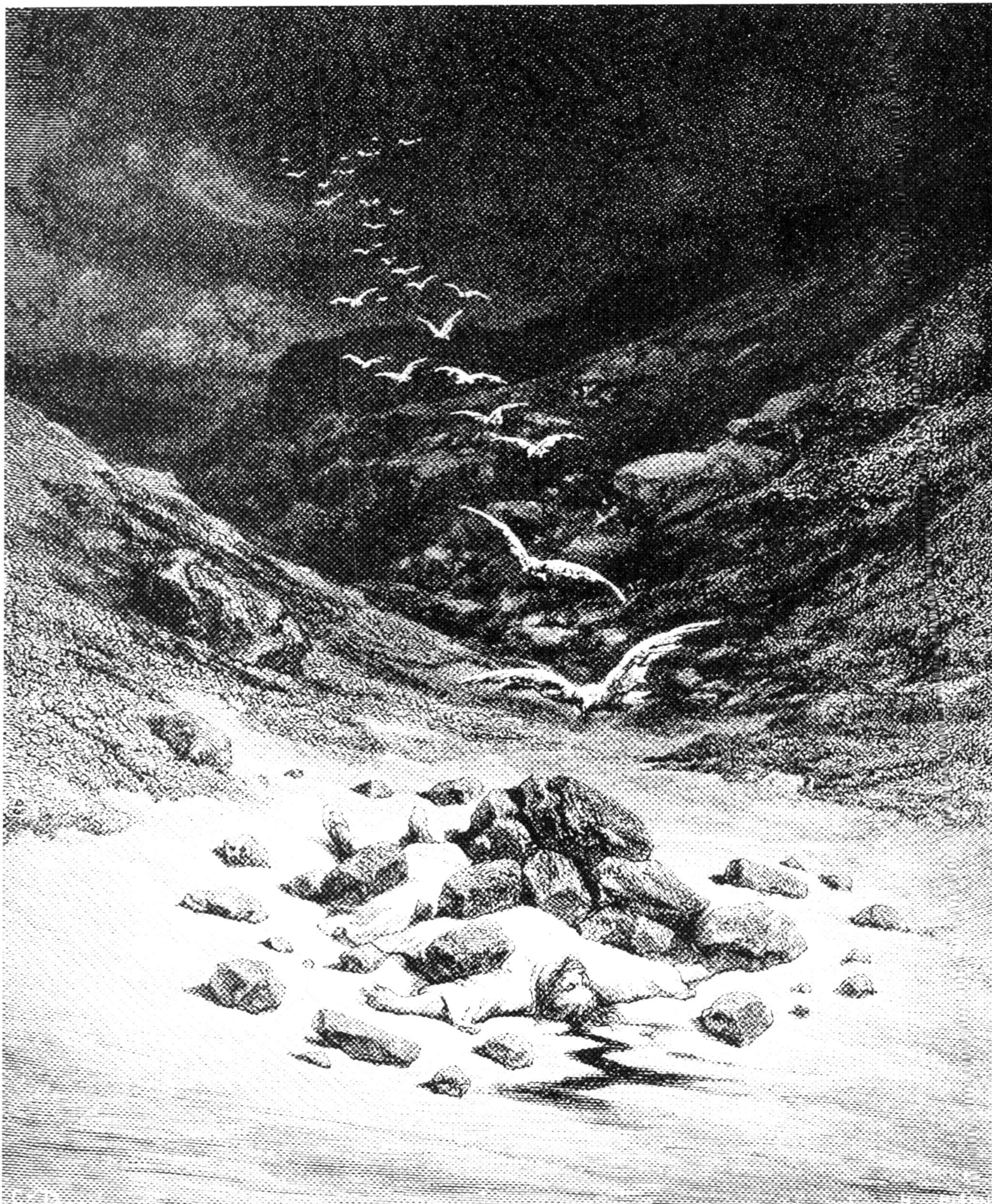

LESSON 2

REJECTED

TROUBLE IN MIND

SCRIPTURE: Joshua 7:1-25
MAIN POINT: Only church leaders are allowed to steal things.

CHILDREN'S ACTIVITY

Have your children move their chairs together to form a circle and choose one child to sit on his chair in the middle of the circle. Blindfold the child sitting in the center and put silver coins (loose change) under his chair. Choose one child in the outer ring to sneak up and see if she can take a coin from under the chair without being heard. If the blindfolded child hears anything, he is to shout, "SINNER!" at the top of his lungs.

DISCUSSION QUESTIONS

- **Look at the picture: What do you think the birds are going to do?** (*Probably eat his eyes or at least poop in them. Good thing he's dead, huh?*)
- **Why does Joshua insist on killing and burning all of Achan's family and his stuff, too?** (*Because when we do something bad, that means our whole family is bad, too.*)
- **Why does Achan try to fool God?** (*He doesn't. He tries to fool Joshua, and God finks on him and tells Joshua to kill Achan.*)
- Ask the children if they know where their mommies and daddies hide money in their houses.
- Ask the children if they've ever been in trouble for something their siblings did. Tell them they're lucky because Achan's family was killed for what he did wrong.

TEACHER HELPS

- Remind the children that God knows *everything*. Even when Achan thought he could get away with something small, God decided not to let him go unpunished. Then a whole bunch of people died—all because of Achan's one little sin.

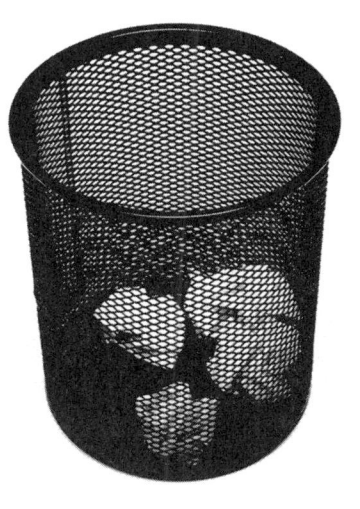

13

REJECTED

- Object Lesson: Tell the children they're going to play a game. Take some blocks (not too many) and dump them on the floor. Tell the children they have to pick them up and put them back in the box. Praise the children for doing it well. Then dump some sugar on the floor. Of course the kids can't get all the sugar, so tell them this is what sin is like: We can never clean up all of it, no matter how hard we try; there will always be a little bit of sin left in our hearts, and that still means God will wipe us out.

CLOSING PRAYER

God, please don't let us get in trouble or let birds poop in our eyes. Amen.

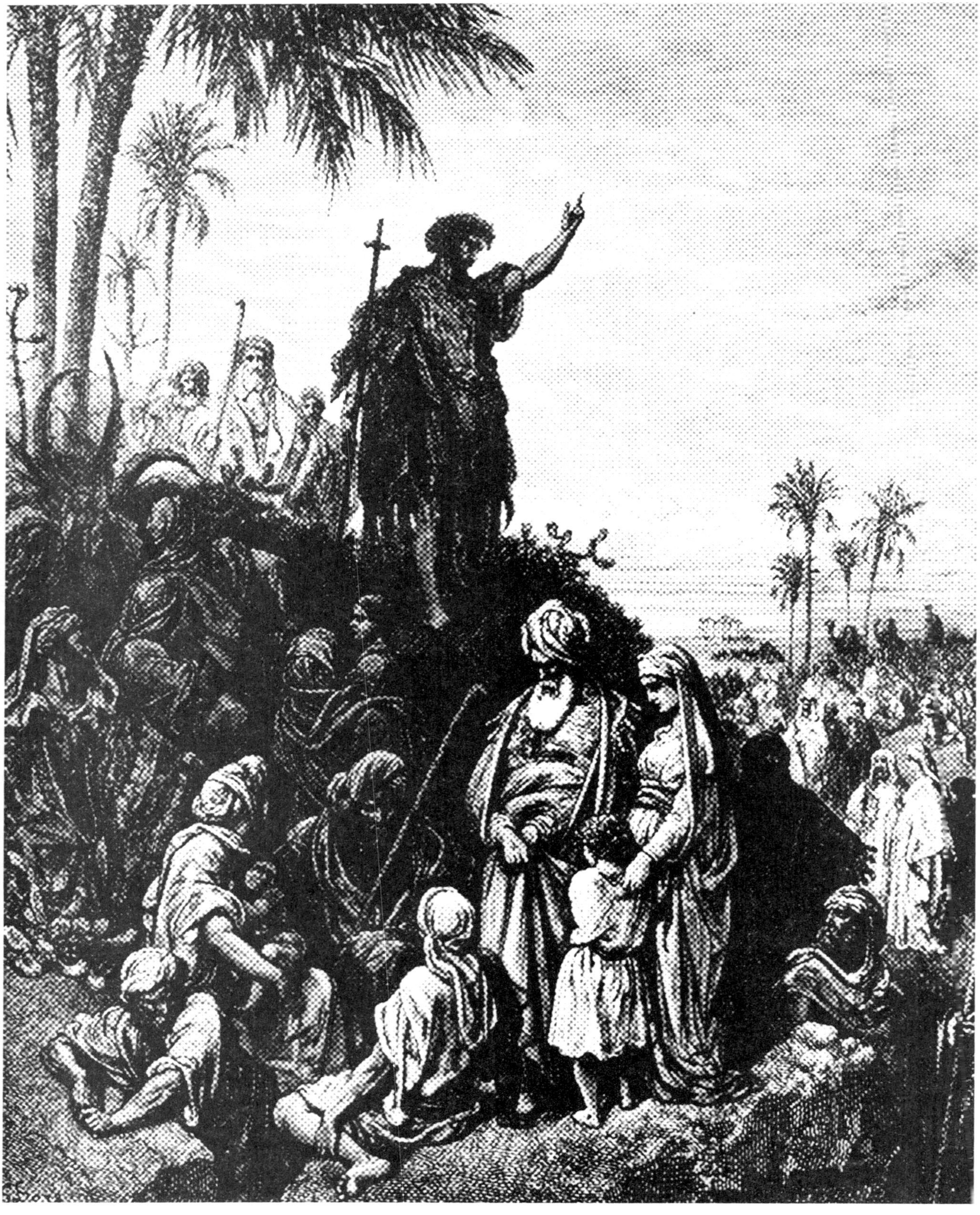

LESSON 3
POVERTY SUCKS

REJECTED

SCRIPTURE: Mark 1:6-7
MAIN POINT: God wants our church to have a new Family Life Center.

CHILDREN'S ACTIVITY

Before teaching this lesson, spend some time capturing grasshoppers that the children can dunk into a jar of honey (which you'll also need to provide) during the lesson. If you can't find grasshoppers in your area, you can probably get a nice supply of crickets from your local pet store. Crickets are harder to handle because they're smaller than grasshoppers. So just pour the honey into the bag of crickets rather than asking the children to dip their crickets into the honey.

DISCUSSION QUESTIONS

- **Why does John the Baptist preach in the wilderness?** (*Mostly he's just trying to witness to the crowds so they'll go to his church in the city.*)

- **How do we know John was Baptist?** (*Because he dunks people under water. If he were a Methodist, they would've called him "John the Sprinkler."*)

- **Is dunking people under water really the best way to baptize them?** (*The best way is to dip people like an Oreo cookie. Just wait for the bubbles to stop, then bring them up quickly before you lose them.*)

- **Do the people really see that light shining above John's head?** (*No. The artist drew it so we'd know which one is John. If the crowds had seen it, they would have asked, "What the h-e-double-hockey-sticks is that light above your head?"*)

- **Some people in the picture look as though they're richer than others, and they don't appear to be listening to John. How come?** (*People to whom God has given lots of money have trouble hearing God's words from a "street preacher." That's why it's important to have our Family Life Center be the best it can be.*) Note: Now would be a good time to get out the offering basket and see if the kids have any change in their pockets.

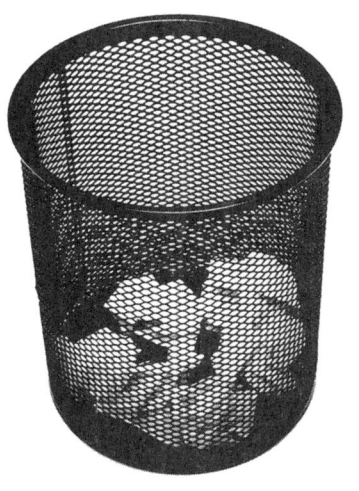

17

REJECTED

• **Why does John have a cross on the end of his staff? Jesus hadn't died yet.** (*John got it from the Family Life Center gift shop. He wanted to show it to Jesus when he came down to the river for his baptism.*)

• **Why does it seem as though the man in the lower-left part of the picture is stuck in the rock formation?** (*He's not stuck. He's leaving to go put his name on the volunteer list for the car wash fundraiser.*) Take this time to pass out the Family Life Center volunteer forms so the children can sign up their parents for your church's fundraising events.

• **Will God really hear us better if we're praying from a new Family Life Center instead of outside in the wilderness?** (*Yes.*)

TEACHER HELPS

• If some of your children resist dipping and eating grasshoppers, tell them it's just like communion—and if they don't try at least one, then Jesus won't come back.

• See if you can get one of the teenagers in the church to volunteer for this session. Instruct him to not bathe or shave for a whole month beforehand. When he comes into the classroom, tell the children that *this* is what John smelled like. Then ask them if they think it's important to take a bath and wear nice clothes before they pray to God.

CLOSING PRAYER

God, if you really want us to do your will—it'll cost you. Amen.

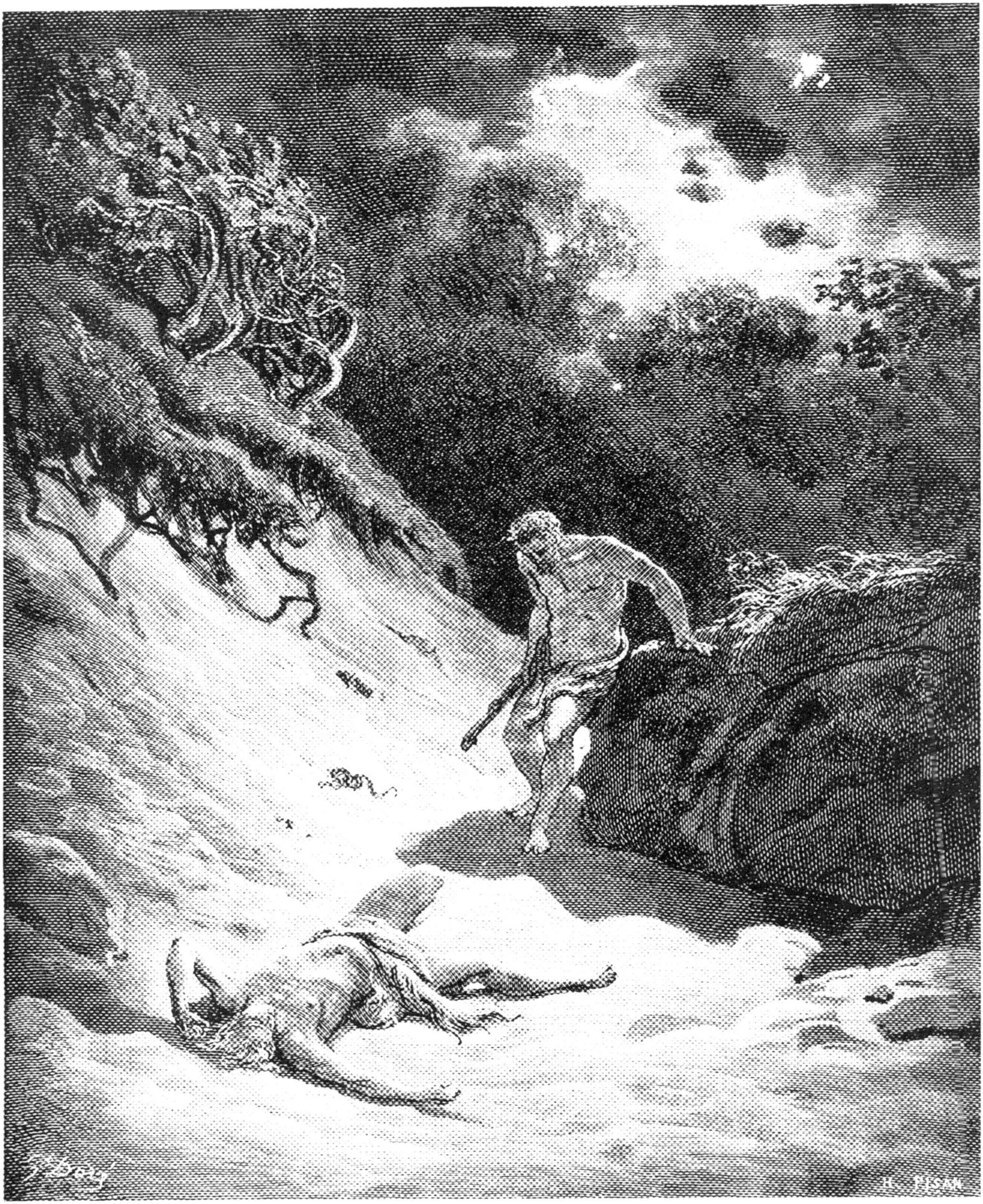

LESSON 4

REJECTED

GUESS WHICH HAND

SCRIPTURE: Genesis 4:8-15
MAIN POINT: It's important for siblings to get along.

CHILDREN'S ACTIVITY

Take a honeydew melon (just a little past ripe is best) and draw a face on the rind. Blindfold the children one at a time and hand them baseball bats. See if any of them can bash open the honeydew. You might want to hold this activity outdoors or on newspaper for easy cleanup.

DISCUSSION QUESTIONS

- **Why does Cain bash Abel's brains in?** (*He believes Adam and Eve like his little brother better.*)

- **Do they?** (*Probably. Whether they admit it or not, most parents really do favor one child over the others.*)

- **Did Cain and Abel fight like siblings of today?** (*Yes, but not as much. They had less to fight over.*)

- **Did Cain try to hide what he did from his parents?** (*Yes, but God knows what he did, and God punished Cain big-time. Remember: God sees everything.*)

- **Is Cain sorry for killing his brother?** (*Yes, but it seems he's only sorry once he gets caught. God wants us to be sorry as soon as we do something bad. This is probably part of the reason why God punished Cain so severely.*)

- **Look at the picture. Do you see the snake? Do you think this could be the same snake that was in the Garden of Eden?** (*Yes. The snake is one of Satan's favorite disguises, but he can appear in any form—including a Democrat.*)

REJECTED

TEACHER HELPS

• Point out that in verses 13 and 14, Cain tries to come up with all kinds of excuses to avoid being banished. Tell the children that in Bible times being "banished" was sort of like being sent to your room without supper.

• Point out that it seems as though Cain and Abel are both wearing some kind of towel in the picture. Tell the children that being naked can make us crazy, and we should always try to wear clothing so we don't go crazy and kill our siblings.

CLOSING PRAYER

God, help us to get along with our siblings so they don't kill us when we're not looking. Amen.

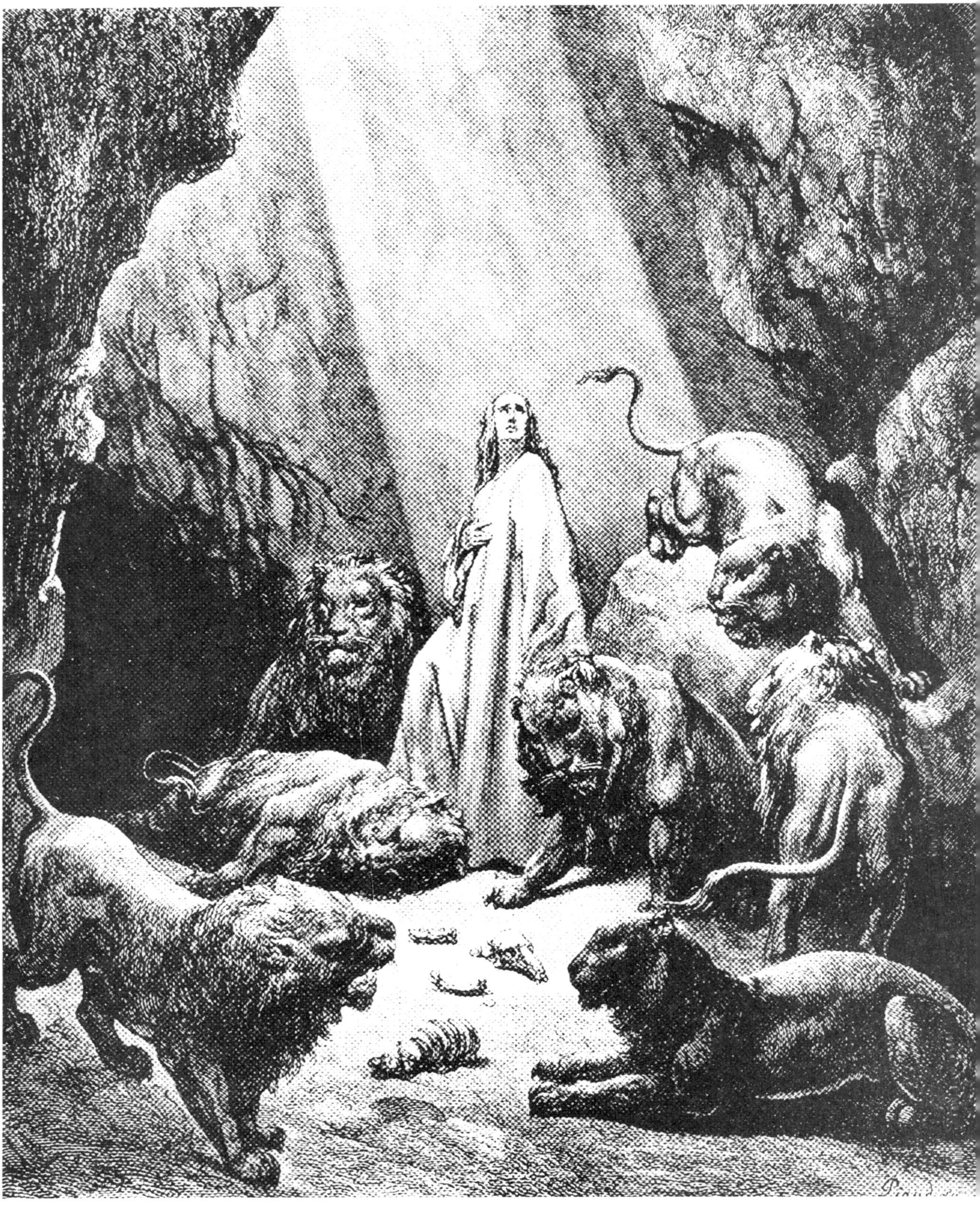

LESSON 5
THE SUN WILL COME OUUUUUUUT TOMORROW

REJECTED

SCRIPTURE: Daniel 6:6-24
MAIN POINT: God likes some people more than others.

CHILDREN'S ACTIVITY

Did you notice in this Bible picture how it looks as though Daniel is going to break into song? (See the spotlight?) Teach the children this song about Daniel's experience (sung to the melody of "Rock Around the Clock"):

> We're the lions in the den
> We'll eat your mom, we'll eat your friends
> We're gonna chew them up morning, noon, and night
> We're gonna chew up Daniel 'til our tummies feel tight
> We're gonna chew him (clap clap), eat poor Daniel tonight.
>
> God sent an angel down to the den
> He said, "Don't eat Daniel at all my friends!
> "God loves him in the morning, noon, and night;
> "If you try to taste him there'll be a big cat fight;
> "Don't eat 'im (clap clap), don't eat poor Daniel tonight!"

DISCUSSION QUESTIONS

• **Did God make the lions into "friendly" lions, or did God just make them feel full so they wouldn't eat Daniel?** (*Take another look at the picture. Daniel seems to be friends with at least a few of them.*)

• **Do these lions sing like the ones in *The Lion King*?** (*No, The Lion King wasn't written when this story took place.*)

• **Why does the king throw Daniel into the lions' den?** (*Because Daniel prays to God.*)

• **Can we get in trouble for praying to God?** (*Only in school, but all they'll do is throw you in the principal's office.*)

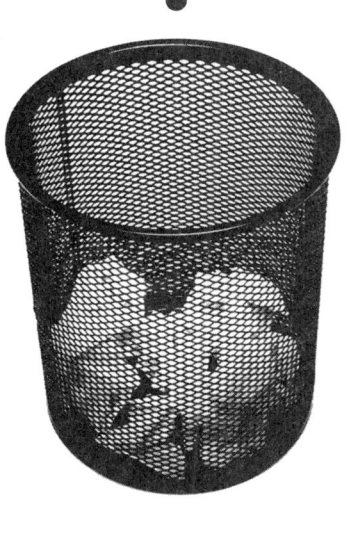

25

REJECTED

• **The advisors don't like Daniel very much. Why not?** (*Because he gave the king better advice. Sometimes we have to work with people who aren't as good as we are, and they may try to hurt us by lying about us to the boss. Then the boss will get mad and try to cut our pay, or write us up on a report, or give us a bad evaluation so we can't get a raise after 20 years of blood, sweat, and tears with the same @%$# publishing company that never listens to our ideas anyway...*)

• **There are bones in the middle of the lions' den. What kinds of animals do you suppose they came from?** (*Probably a puppy or a kitty.*)

TEACHER HELPS

• Point out that at the end of the Bible story, the king had his advisors, their wives, and their children thrown into the pit to be devoured by the lions. Ask the children if they think they might get in trouble for something mommy or daddy did. Then ask them to tell you what it was so you can "pray about it."

CLOSING PRAYER

God, please help us to be honest at all times so we won't get eaten by lions. Amen.

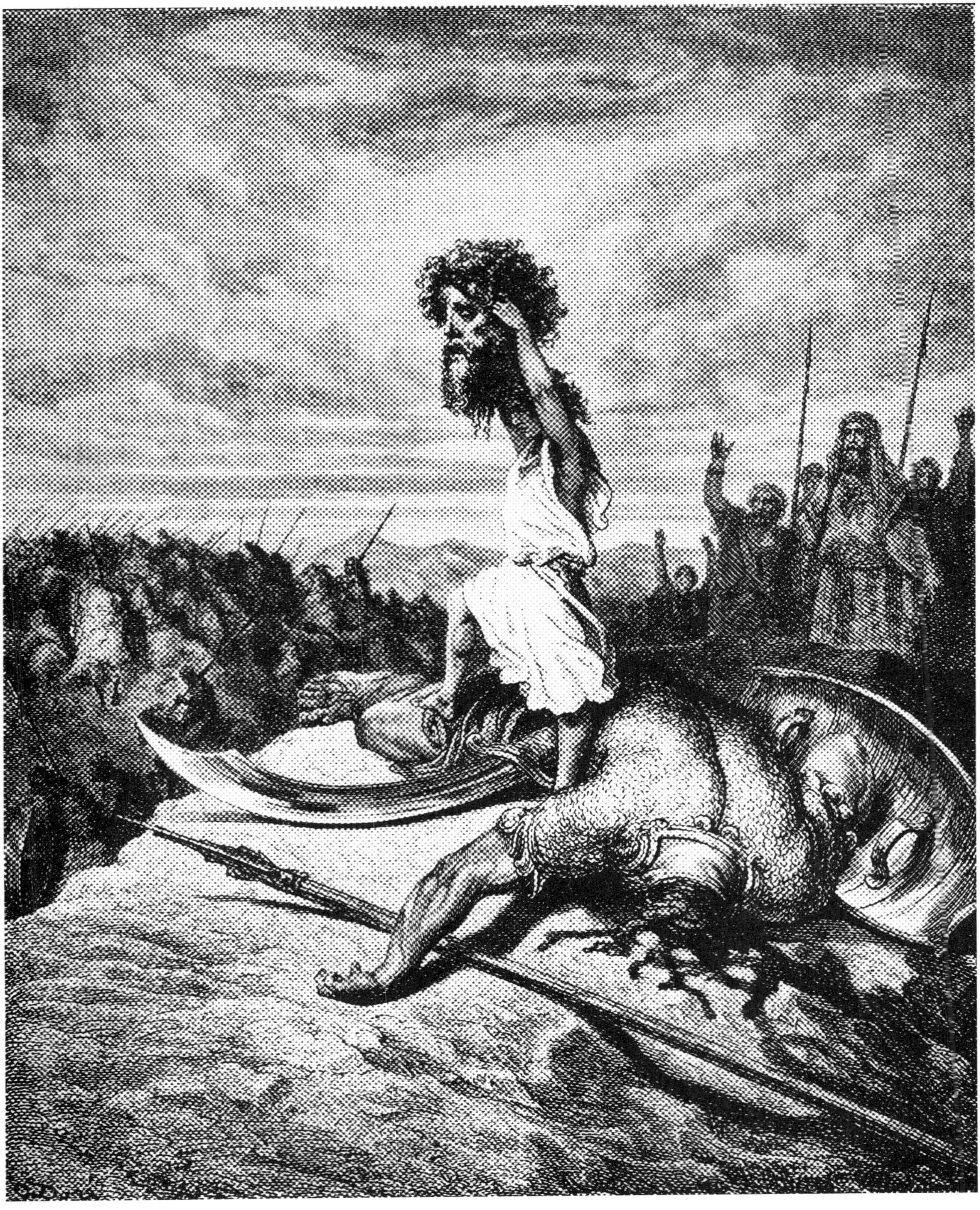

LESSON 6

REJECTED

GOOOOOOAAAALLLLLLLLLLL!

SCRIPTURE: 1 Samuel 17:20-50
MAIN POINT: Nobody messes with God.

CHILDREN'S ACTIVITY

Here's a little game to show the children how well God listens. You'll need a dodge ball or other playground ball. (Don't use stones for this game.) Have one of the children be Goliath; you get to be David. Have the student stand near the wall; you stand about 10 to 15 feet away. Tell the student she's allowed to hurl insults at you for 60 seconds. She can say anything she wants—except profanity. When she's finished insulting you, bow your head in silent prayer, then throw the ball at her as hard as you can. (Remember: David aimed for Goliath's head.) Have extra balls on hand in case she's a quick ducker.

DISCUSSION QUESTIONS

- Why do you think David doesn't want to use King Saul's armor? (*Because Saul is an old man, and the armor probably smells bad.*)

- David nails Goliath with the first stone. Why do you think he takes five stones with him? (*Because he doubts God's plan; God got him back later in life, though.*)

- David doesn't kill Goliath with the stone; he simply knocks Goliath out and then hacks off his head. But wouldn't Jesus have wanted David to help Goliath up and tend to his wounds? (*Well, Jesus wasn't there.*)

- What does David do with Goliath's head? (*The Bible says David takes it, along with Goliath's weapons, to Jerusalem. But David did have a habit of giving body parts to King Saul as gifts—1 Samuel 18:27—so one can assume…*)

- Is Goliath the only giant in the Bible? (*No. There was a race of giants called the Anakites. They're mentioned a few times. Most of them died from head injuries. Their descendants are now centers for pro basketball teams.*)

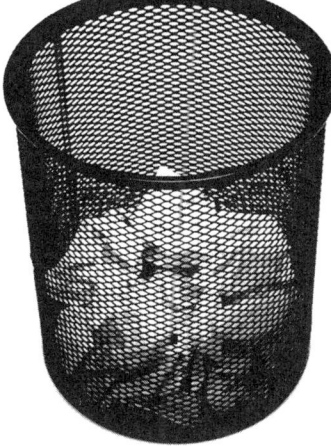

REJECTED

TEACHER HELPS

• Point out that the figure off to the right in the picture is probably King Saul. He isn't cheering. Saul got very jealous of David over the years, and they fought a lot. David once cut off a piece of Saul's robe while he was going to the bathroom.

• Remind the children that they shouldn't throw rocks at people who pick on them, especially at school. They're supposed to do what Jesus did—not what David did. If they argue about this, read the passage about David dancing in his ephod (2 Samuel 6:12-15). Then ask, **You wouldn't want to dance in an ephod, would you, Jimmy?**

• Point out the goal posts pictured just to David's right (behind Saul). Explain that in Old Testament times, it was a tradition to play a game similar to what we'd call soccer. But instead of using a ball, they kicked around the heads of their enemies.

CLOSING PRAYER

God, help us open a can of you-know-what on all of your enemies. Amen.

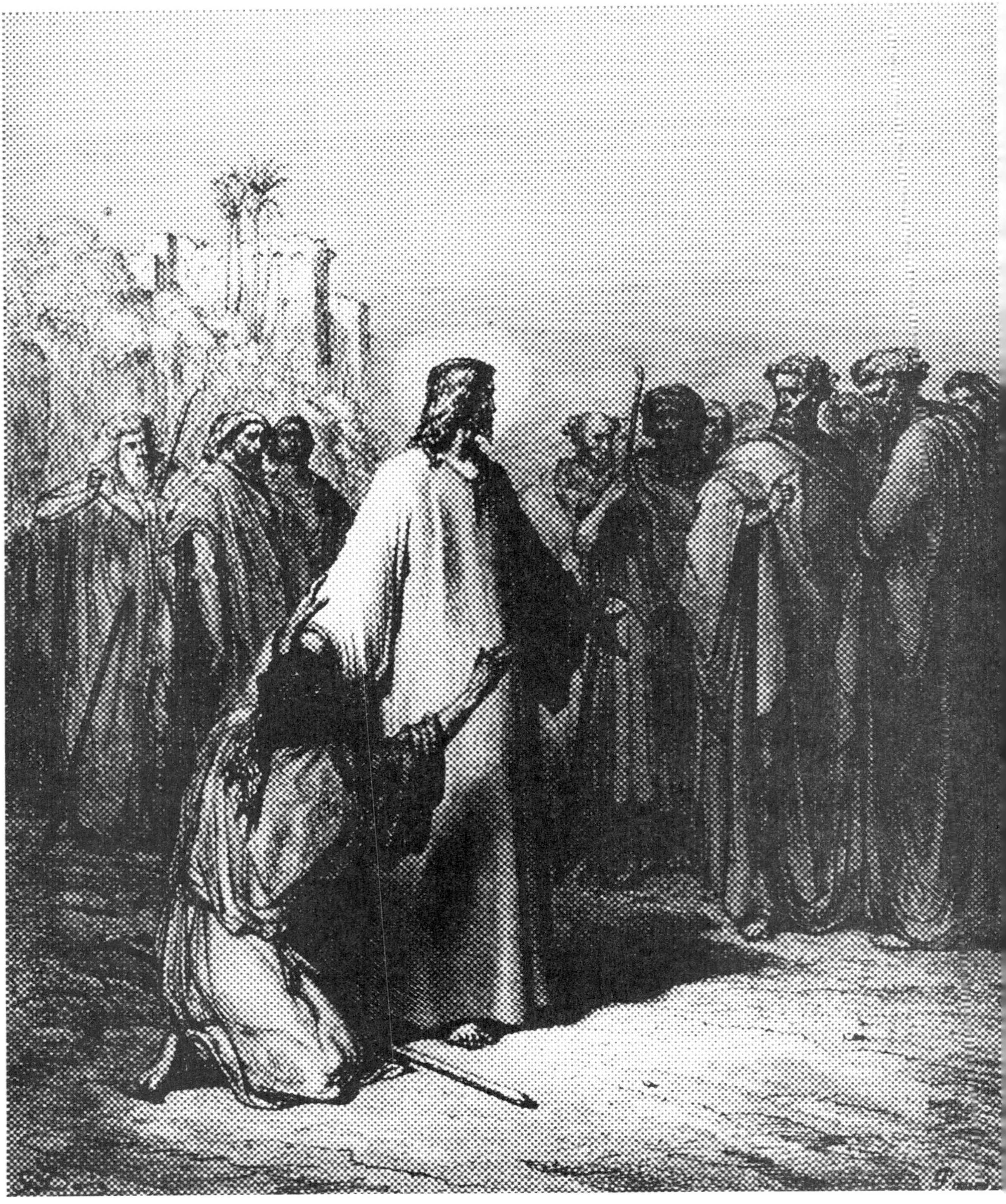

LESSON 7
JESUS FOR DUMMIES

REJECTED

SCRIPTURE: Matthew 9:32-33 (KJV)
MAIN POINT: Jesus loves us even when we do dumb things.

CHILDREN'S ACTIVITY

Before the class arrives, use a sharp knife to carefully cut open the bottom of a Twinkie and remove some of the sponge cake. Next, scoop out the cream filling. Replace it with tuna salad. Put the piece of sponge cake back and set the Twinkie on a plate next to an untouched Twinkie. Tell the students you need two volunteers to help you figure out which Twinkie contains an unpleasant surprise. Of course, you'll need volunteers. Tell the children to count down 3…2…1…GO! and have the volunteers grab a Twinkie and bite into it. Ask the volunteer who bit into the tuna-salad Twinkie if she feels dumb now.

Then remind the students who giggle that *both* volunteers knew they might get a nasty surprise, but they both chose to be dumb anyway.

DISCUSSION QUESTIONS

- **What dumb things do you think the dumb guy in our Bible story might have done?**
- **What are some dumb things you've done?**
- **What are some dumb things Mommy or Daddy have done?** (*Again, you only want to know this information so you can pray for the children's parents.*)
- **What are some dumb things Jesus did?** (*This is a trick question because Jesus didn't do dumb things; he wasn't like us.*)

TEACHING HELPS

- Show the children the picture. Point out that Jesus seems to be turning away from the dumb man. Tell the children that Jesus will turn away from them, too, if they keep on being dumb.

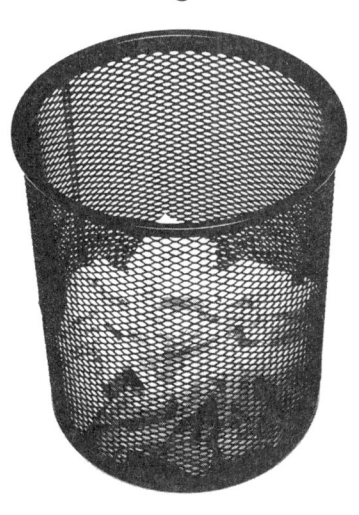

REJECTED

- Show them how Jesus' head is glowing in the picture. Explain that it's glowing because Jesus is smart—not dumb like them.

- Point out the stick lying in front of the dumb man. Then show or read to the children Proverbs 10:13 (NLT), which says dumb people get beaten with sticks.

- Remind the students that Jesus loves even really dumb people—as long as they try to be smarter the next time.

CLOSING PRAYER

God, forgive us when we do dumb things. Amen.

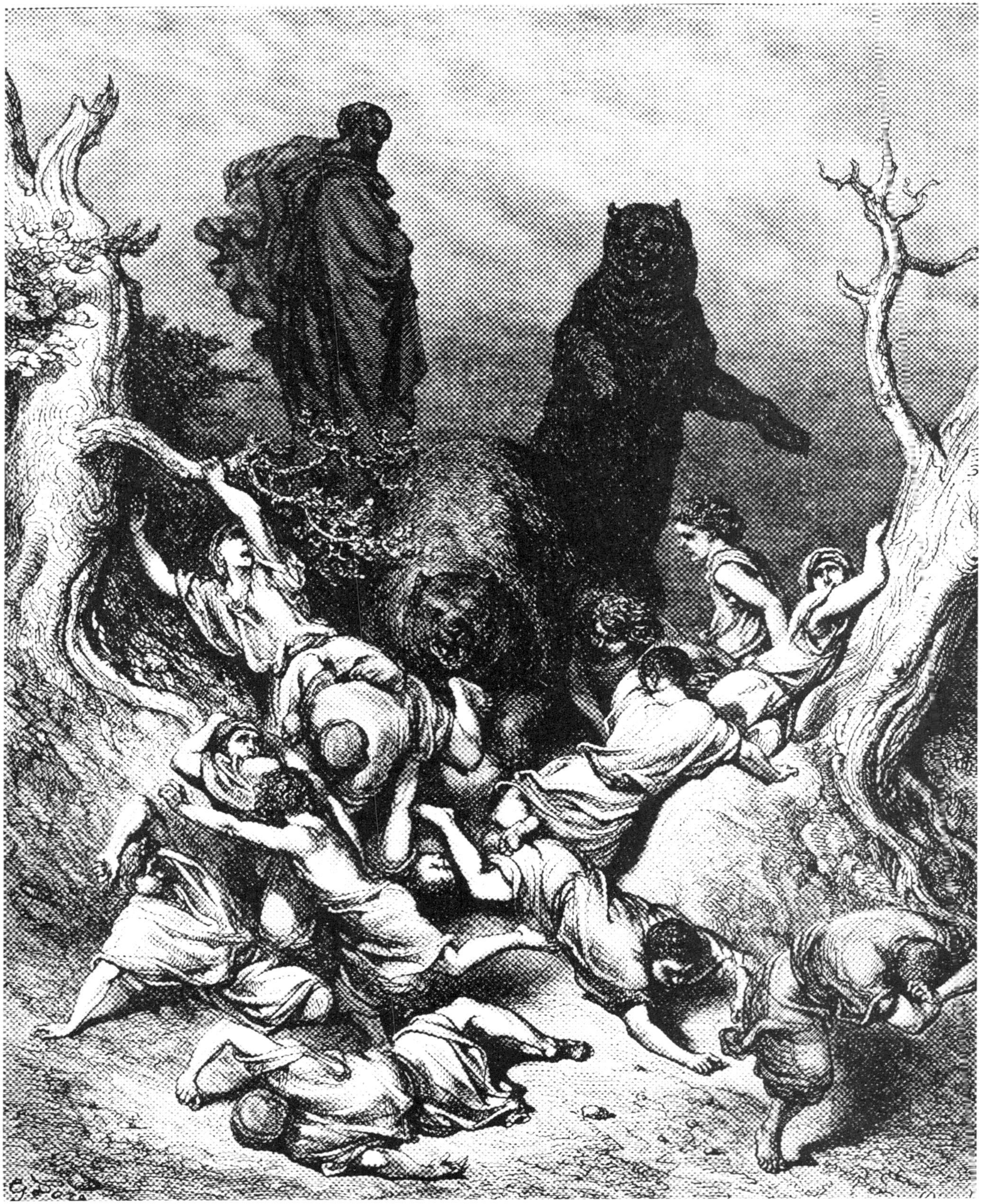

LESSON 8
HERE A BEAR, THERE A BEAR

REJECTED

SCRIPTURE: 2 Kings 2:23-24 (KJV)
MAIN POINT: Respect your elders.

CHILDREN'S ACTIVITY

Teach the children this song about Elisha (sung to the melody of "Old McDonald"):

> Poor Elisha had no hair, E-I-E-I-O
> But his best friends were two big bears, E-I-E-I-O
> With a "Grrrr! Grrrr!" here, and a "Grrrr! Grrrr!" there
> Here a "Grrrrr!" there a "Grrrrrrr!" Everywhere a "Grrrrrrr! Grrrrrrrrrrr!"
> Poor Elisha had no hair, E-I-E-I-O

> The children laughed at his bald head, E-I-E-I-O
> He told the bears, and they wound up dead, E-I-E-I-O
> With a "Hellllllp Meee!" here and an "OWW! OWWWWWW!" there
> Here an "Owwwwww!" there a "Heeeeeeelp!" Everywhere an "Oww! Hellllp!"
> The children laughed at his bald head, E-I-E-I-O

OPTIONAL ACTIVITY

If you have time, add the following verse, inserting the name of one of your students in the blank. If you're running short on time, just use the names of those kids who've been disrespectful to their elders.

> They chewed up _____ and said "Yum! Yum!" E-I-E-I-O
> "Let's eat some more and have some fun," E-I-E-I-O
> With a "Hellllllp Meee!" here and an "OWW! OWWWWWW!" there,

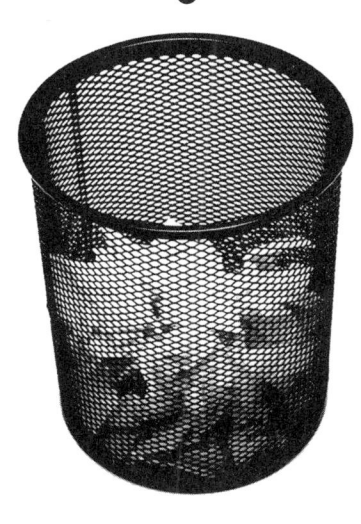

37

REJECTED

SUNDAY SCHOOL LESSONS

Here an "Owwwwww!" There a "Heeeeeeelp!" Everywhere an "Oww! Hellllp!"
They chewed up _____ and said "Yum! Yum!" E-I-E-I-O!

DISCUSSION QUESTIONS

• **Why do the children make fun of Elisha's bald head?** (*Because they weren't good Christian children.*)

• **Didn't they have toupees back then?** (*Yes, many men wore wigs. But the wigs were made of horse hair, and they smelled bad when it rained.*)

• **Where does Elisha learn to speak Bear?** (*He doesn't speak Bear. He speaks English, and God let the bears understand Elisha.*)

• **Why are there two mommy bears and not three bears, like in Goldilocks and the Three Bears?** (*God's trying to make a point about marriage.*)

• **Does God have hair?** (*Yes, lots of it. It's white, and it hangs down past his shoulders. He also has a white beard. Elisha has no hair because he's getting old.*)

TEACHER HELPS

• Show the picture and ask, **Do any of the children in this picture look like children in this room?**

• Say, **Look at Elisha in the picture. Does it look as though he has hair?** (*It's hard to tell, isn't it? Maybe we shouldn't call our elders names until we're sure they deserve it.*)

CLOSING PRAYER

God, help us to remember that we're all bear meat unless we love Jesus. Amen.

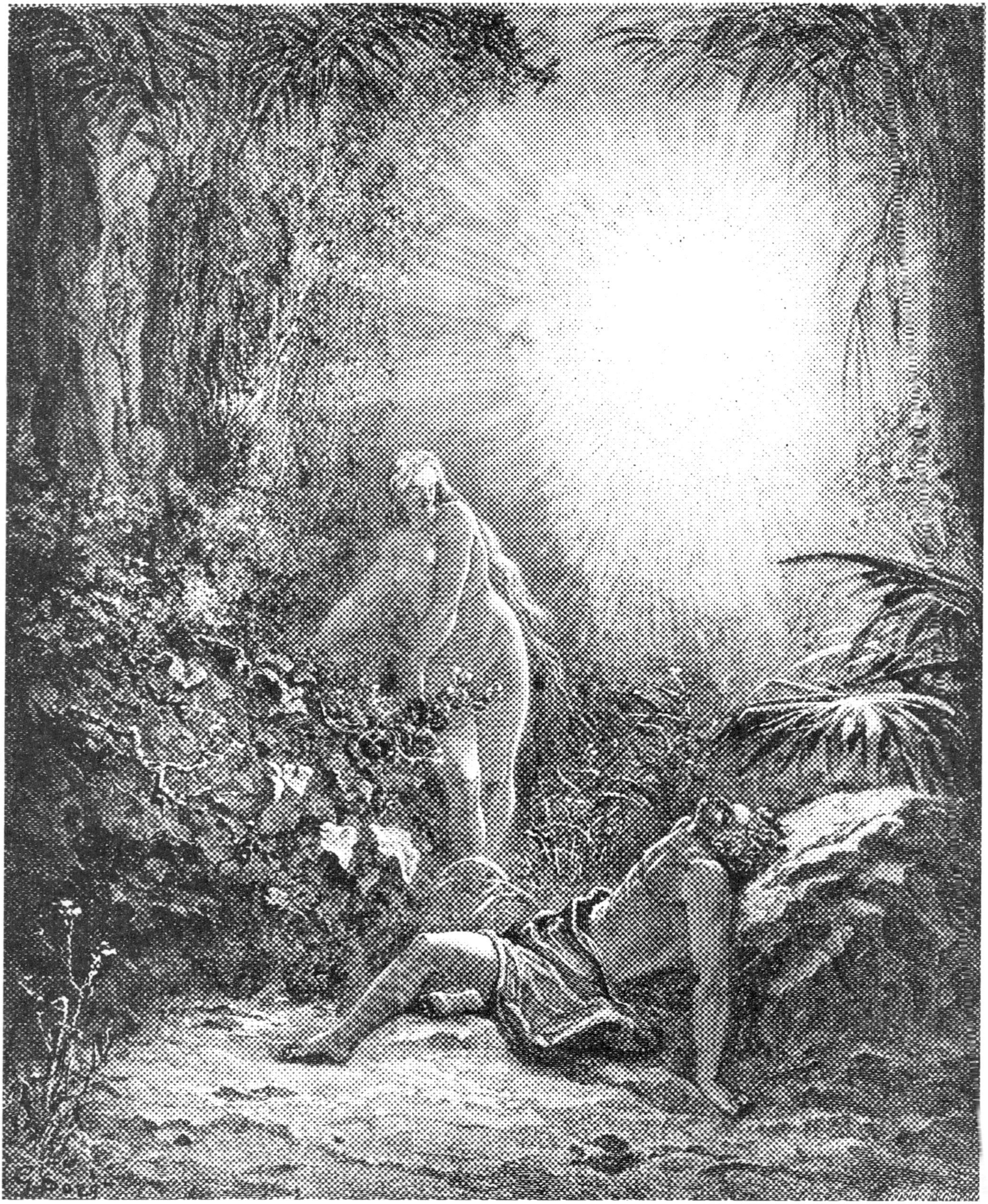

LESSON 9
ADAM TAKES A RIBBING

REJECTED

SCRIPTURE: Genesis 2:21-3:24
MAIN POINT: Even though she lived a long time ago, most of today's problems can be blamed on Eve.

CHILDREN'S ACTIVITY

See if you can get some ribs from your local barbecue place. (Tell management it's for Jesus; maybe they'll let you have some for free.) Hand the ribs to the children (be sure to have some wet wipes on hand for clean up). Tell them they have five minutes to fashion their ribs into a human being. After a few minutes of unsuccessful attempts, tell the kids it's okay if they can't do it because: 1) Only God can make humans, and 2) These are pig ribs, so there's no way they could turn into human beings anyway.

DISCUSSION QUESTIONS

• **Why doesn't God make Eve out of the mud like he does with Adam?** (*Because God wants Eve to know she's part of Adam, and she has to do what Adam says, just like his other body parts.*)

• **Why does Adam have to sleep?** (*Would you want to be awake for this?*) Optional Idea: Have a large knife stashed under your chair or out of the children's view. Now pull it out and pretend to ask for a volunteer.

• **Do men get to be in charge of everything since God made Adam first?** (*Yes.*)

• Point out in the picture how it appears as though Adam is taking a nap, and Eve is coming to wake him up. Ask the kids how many of them have ever seen what happens when Mommy tries to wake up Daddy too early…

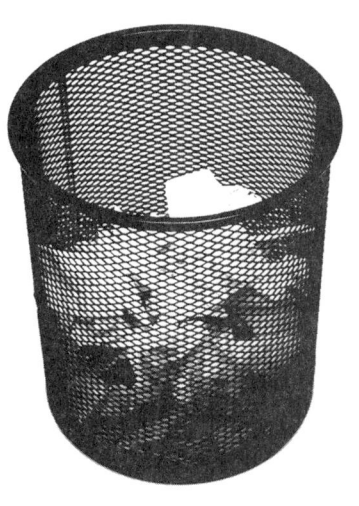

REJECTED

- Why does God put the apple tree in the garden in the first place? Couldn't he have just kept the garden free of temptation? (*God wants to see how well Adam "manages" his wife. Adam doesn't do a very good job, does he?*)

TEACHER HELPS

- Point out to the children that back then rib removal was a major operation, not just something supermodels do to look skinnier. Say—**God removed Adam's rib without any modern-day equipment. Isn't God wonderful?**

- Make sure the children know that even though Adam and Eve were naked, that was sort of okay because there wasn't anyone else around to see them. Adam and Eve finally cover up before leaving their home. Remind the children that they should always dress appropriately when they leave their homes as well.

- Some of the children may know certain families where it seems as though the mother is the one in charge. Encourage your students to love these families anyway and to always remember: "Our church does it God's way."

CLOSING PRAYER

God, even though it's Eve's fault, we're all just a bunch of sinners. Please forgive Eve and forgive us, too. Amen.

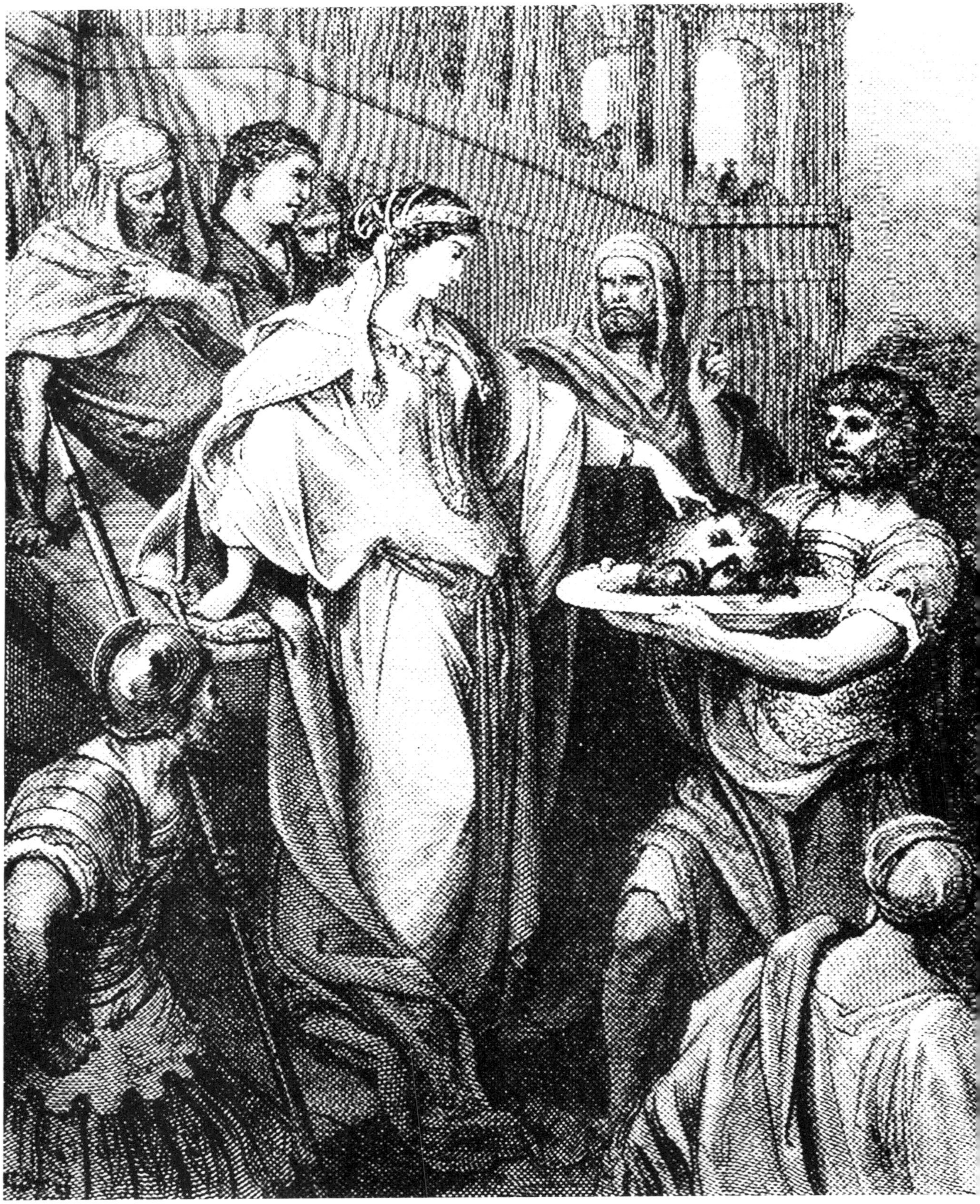

LESSON 10

REJECTED

HEAD, SHOULDERS, KNEES, AND TOES (KNEES AND TOES)...

SCRIPTURE: Matthew 14:1-12
MAIN POINT: Good girls don't.
OTHER MAIN POINT: Good girls don't ask for outlandish birthday gifts.

CHILDREN'S ACTIVITY

Provide each child with a paper plate, then set out some strawberry jam, vanilla ice cream (not soft-serve), jelly beans, red licorice, and chocolate-covered grasshoppers (these are optional, of course; you may be able to find some at your local novelty store). Each kid should make a small puddle of strawberry jam on his paper plate. After you've placed a round scoop of vanilla ice cream in the center of each child's puddle of jam, ask the children to make faces on their scoops of ice cream, using the jelly beans and red licorice. The chocolate grasshoppers can be used as a garnish.

DISCUSSION QUESTIONS

• Does Herodias' daughter really ask for the head of John the Baptist as her birthday gift? (*No, it's really Herod's birthday, but he offers her a present anyway.*)

• Why does Herod offer her a present? (*Because she danced like a hussy.*)

• Why does she want John's head? (*Actually her mother wants it because John told her she's a hussy.*)

• Why is the girl touching John's head in the picture? (*One of the guards said, "Where's the temple?" Herodias' daughter wasn't very smart; that's why she danced like a hussy.*)

• Do all stupid girls act like hussies? (*Yes.*)

• Why does it appear as though the man in the lower-left part of the picture is wearing a skirt? (*It was probably quite a party.*)

• What kind of games did they play at King Herod's party? (*Ask your mommy and daddy.*)

REJECTED

TEACHER HELPS

• Point out how provocatively Herodias' daughter is dressed. (None of the other men in the picture seem upset that there's a head sitting on a plate.)

• Point out that Jesus is very upset—so upset he cries—when he finds out what Herodias' daughter requests for a present. Explain that Jesus still cries when young ladies ask for selfish gifts.

CLOSING PRAYER

Jesus, we're sorry we make you cry. Please help us to use our heads. Amen.

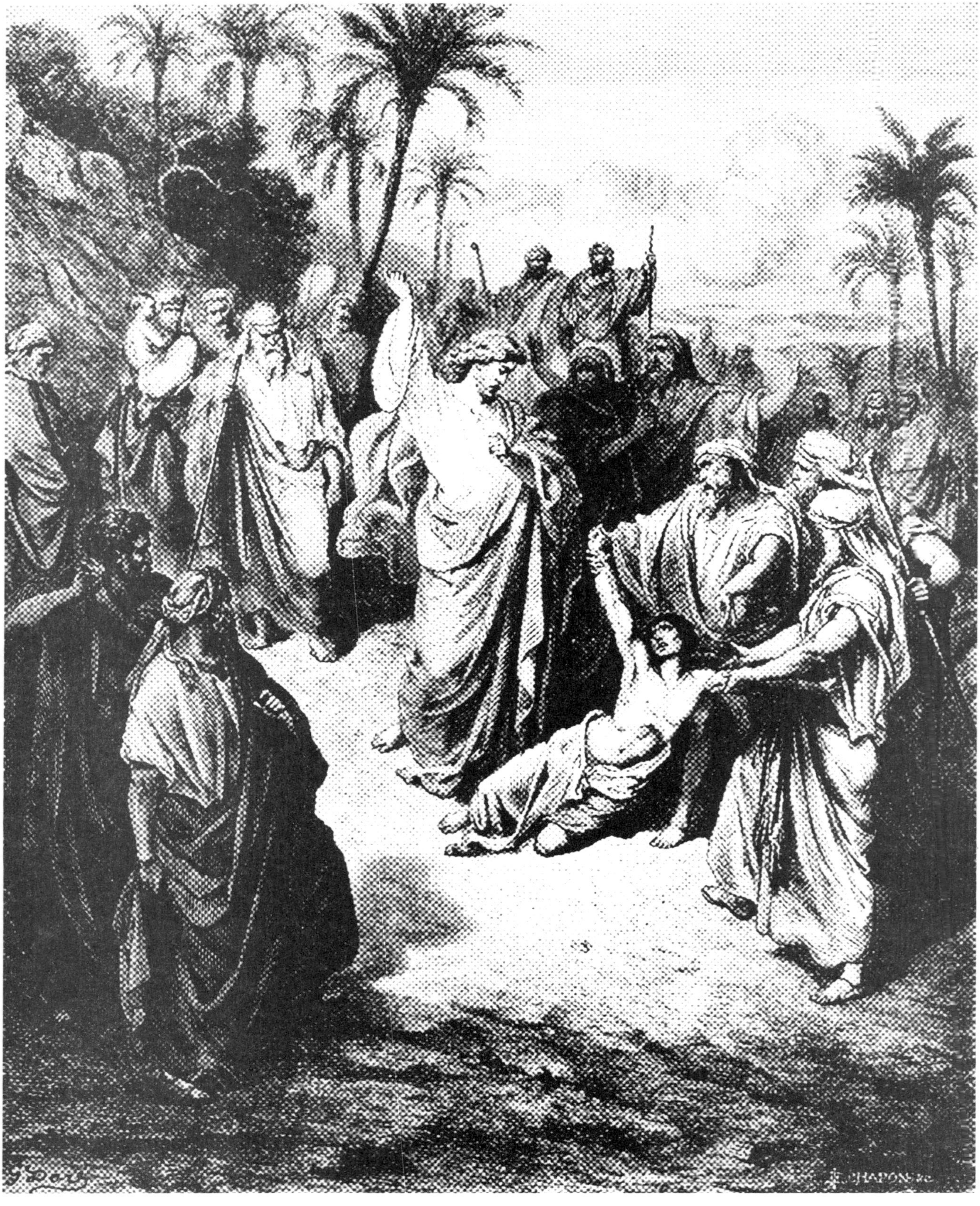

LESSON 11

REJECTED

DANCE, YOU SON OF GOD, DANCE!

SCRIPTURE: Matthew 17:14-18
MAIN POINT: Jesus shows the crowd that he can party with the best of them.

CHILDREN'S ACTIVITY

Select one of the more Christian-y teenagers from the church youth group to come and play some of today's more popular Christian music. Tell the children they should dance just like Jesus did. Don't let them quit. If the children say they're getting tired of dancing, tell them they have to keep dancing until you say *stop*. Say something like, **Did Jesus get tired?** If they start to wear down, serve double shots of espresso as part of the Sunday school snack. Keep them dancing until the last child falls over.

You can also teach the children to sing "YHWH" (to the chorus of "YMCA"). Have the children throw their arms in the air to make the letter shapes, too!

> Y-H-W-H
> Y-H-W-H
> You can get yourself saved, though your friends think you're odd
> You can dance with the Son of God…

DISCUSSION QUESTIONS

• **Do you think Jesus danced a lot?** (*Probably not. Most of the time dancing should be done with two people, and Jesus didn't do that.*)

• Point out the man in the picture, just to the left of Jesus, who seems to have brought a child. **Is it okay for children to dance the "Jesus dance"?** (*Yes, but they can only do the first part.*)

• **When can children dance the part where they fall into the fire or water?** (*When they're married.*)

• **Why are the men in the picture holding the man's arms?** (*The man was attempting to crowd surf and fell because there weren't enough people to catch him.*)

49

REJECTED

TEACHER HELPS

• Read the Scripture and explain to the children that "The Lunatic" was a special dance people did in Jesus' time and that the young man in the picture who fell was probably on drugs.

• Ask the children if they've ever sung or heard the song "Lord of the Dance." (*Not* the *Riverdance* show on PBS, but the song many children learn at summer camp.) Tell the children that Jesus in this picture is probably trying to "lead them all in the dance said he."

• Point out the man in the lower-left corner of the picture. Say, **See how he's trying to do the "Jesus Dance"?** (*Actually he's doing something closer to the "Satan Dance," and God will probably smite him with a lion later on.*)

CLOSING PRAYER

God, help us to get down and funky the way Jesus did. Amen.

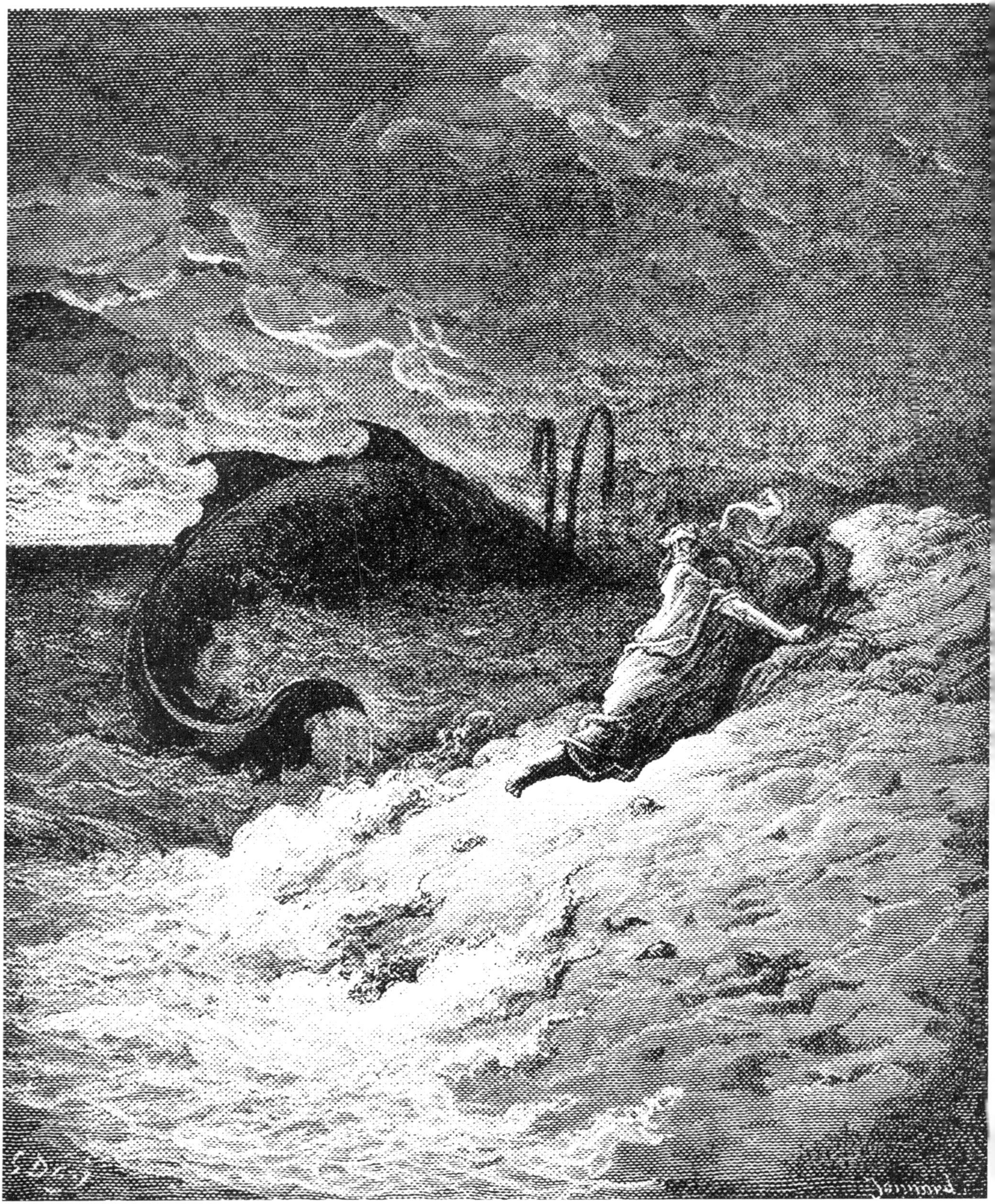

LESSON 12

REJECTED

PLOP PLOP, FIZZ FIZZ

SCRIPTURE: Jonah 2:1-10
MAIN POINT: God can talk to animals.

CHILDREN'S ACTIVITY

Think about what Jonah had to eat for those three days when he was in the belly of the fish. Mostly other fish! Before teaching this lesson, purchase some frozen fish sticks and mix them with some of the children's favorite foods. Examples: Peanut Butter and Jellyfish (PB&J with mashed fish sticks), S'more Fish (classic s'mores, but with fish sticks instead of marshmallows), Fish in the Ocean (blue Jell-O in a clear plastic cup with submerged fish sticks), Sea Dogs (fish sticks in hot dog buns with mustard and ketchup), and De-baitable Dinner (gummy worms wrapped around fish sticks).

DISCUSSION QUESTIONS

• Notice in the Bible passage how the first thing Jonah does after he's swallowed is pray. Do you think Jonah was finally getting the idea? (*No. The first thing Jonah does is list a bunch of things God already knows.*)

• Why doesn't God send another ship or simply turn Jonah's ship around? (*Because the big fish wasn't all that busy, and because God wants Jonah to smell like fish vomit when he gets to Nineveh.*)

• The creature in the picture looks like a giant catfish, not a whale. Why? (*The Bible never uses the word "whale." Because there wasn't a lot of deep sea fishing being done back then, catfish and other fish, such as trout, were allowed to grow to gigantic sizes.*)

• The Bible says God "commanded" the fish. Does God talk to fish the same way Aquaman does on the cartoons, or does God actually go down under the water and talk to the fish in "fish-ese"? (*Fish don't have ears, so God must have communicated by telepathy; but it probably doesn't make the same sound as Aquaman's telepathy.*)

• Does God talk to other animals? (*Only Christian ones.*)

53

REJECTED

TEACHER HELPS

• Point out that the Bible says Jonah is in the fish's belly and was then vomited up. All this happened because Jonah tells God *no*—something we should never do. Who knows what God will send to eat us?

CLOSING PRAYER

God, help us always to listen and do what we're told so we don't get vomited from the belly of a Christian animal. Amen.

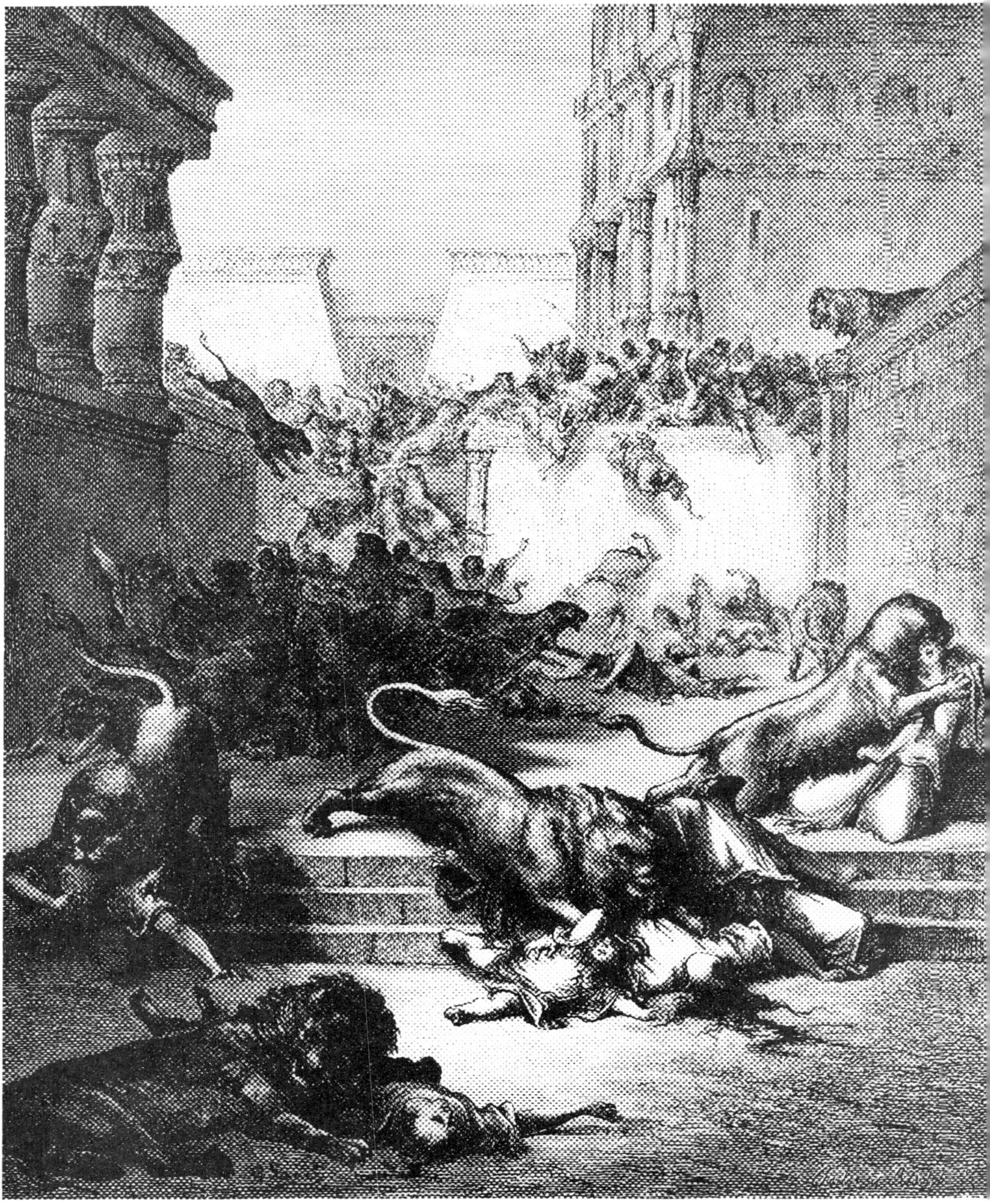

LESSON 13
REJECTED
THE NEW KID IN TOWN

SCRIPTURE: 2 Kings 17:22-27
MAIN POINT: When you move to a new town, find a new church quick!

CHILDREN'S ACTIVITY

Practice roaring with the children. Play a recording of a real lion's roar, if you can find one. Explain that God has specific instructions for the people in this passage, but they don't pay attention. So God sends the lions to scare them. Tell the children that the next time they go to "big people's church," they're allowed to sneak up behind the people sitting in front of them and ROAR! at the top of their lungs (especially if it looks as though the person isn't paying attention).

DISCUSSION QUESTIONS

• **Why is God mad at the Assyrians?** (*They aren't really Assyrians. They moved there from other places. They're supposed to learn about the local church customs and don't.*)

• **What are they doing instead?** (*They're worshiping other gods instead of the one true God.*)

• **So God sends lions to eat them?** (*Not all of them; the Bible says "some of the people."*)

• **How many is that?** (*When your mother says you have to eat "some" vegetables in order to get dessert—it was like that.*)

• **How come ALL the newcomers aren't eaten?** (*Some of them were on their way to church instead of sleeping in.*)

• **The lions eat the people who're sleeping in?** (*Yes. And those watching TV instead of going to Sunday school.*)

• **How are the chewed-up people supposed to know any better?** (*When you move to a new town, the first thing you must do is find a church. You have to do this before you find a school, and definitely before you find a good pizza place.*)

REJECTED

- If we move to a new town, will God send lions to chew on us if we don't go to a church? (*Yes.*)

- What if our parents don't want to go? (*Wake them up on Sunday morning—jump up and down on their beds and yell, "Let's go to church! Let's go to church!" Remember: you could be saving your mommies' and daddies' lives.*)

TEACHER HELPS

- Show the children the picture and ask if any of the people in the picture look like their own mommy or daddy.

- Point out that most movies and cartoons don't show lions eating people. Make sure the children understand that the lions in the picture are God's special lions who do what they're told and don't sing.

- Point out what looks like a tornado in the background, just like the one in *The Wizard of Oz*. Ask the children if they remember which one of Dorothy's new friends tried to eat her doggie.

CLOSING PRAYER

God, please don't ever let us move away; but if we do, remind us to find a new church as soon as we can. Amen.

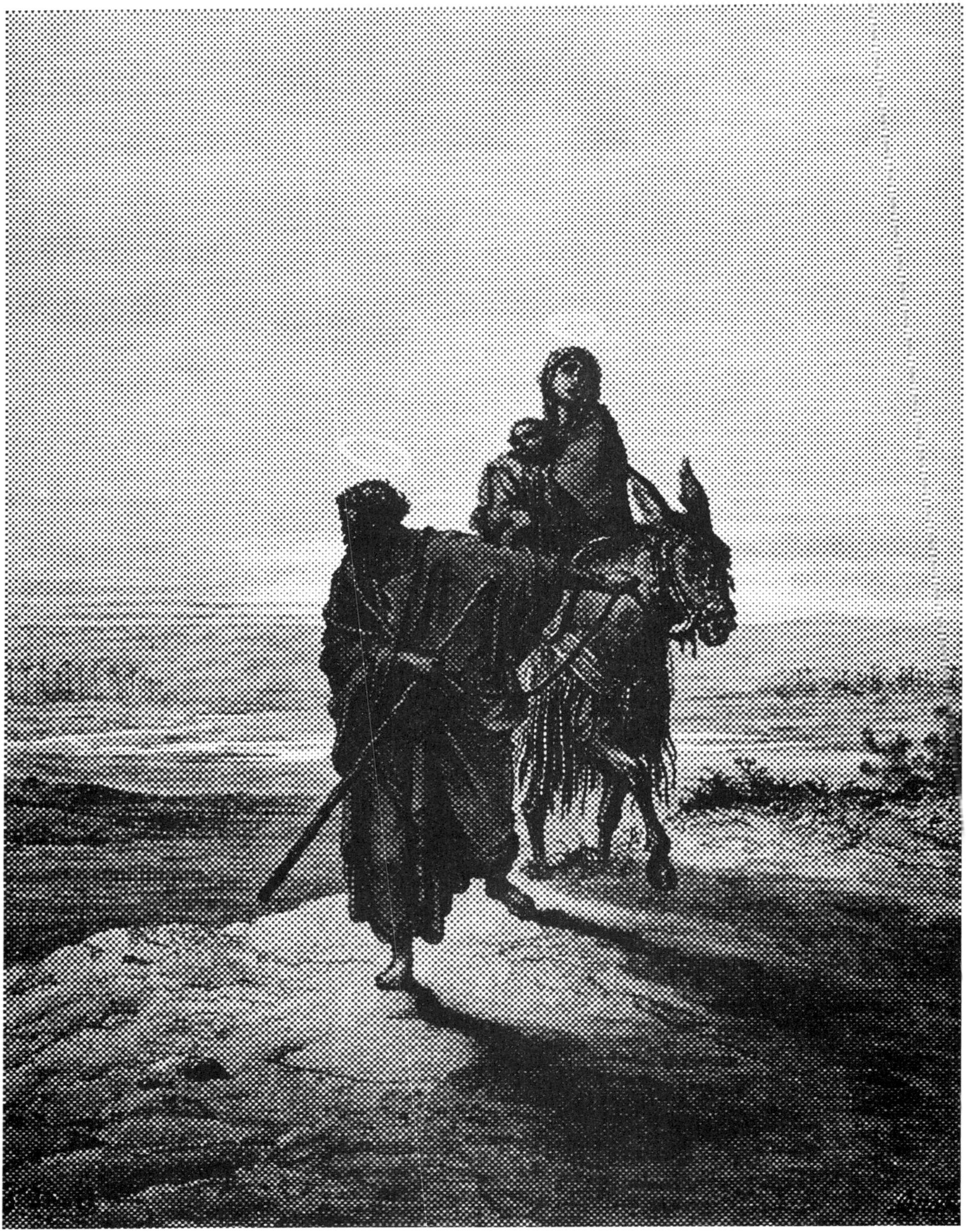

LESSON 14

REJECTED

IT'S MOVING DAY!

SCRIPTURE: Matthew 2:13-14
MAIN POINT: It sucks to move.

CHILDREN'S ACTIVITY

Using tinsel left over from Christmas, make a halo for each child. Put them on the children's heads and tell them they can't take them off for a whole week. They even have to sleep and bathe while wearing their halos. Talk about how hard it must have been to have halos like Mary and Joseph did. Explain that God wants us to act as though we have halos over our heads all the time—even if we can't see them. Make sure they know Jesus is always watching us to see if we're acting as though our halos are still shining.

DISCUSSION QUESTIONS

• **Why doesn't Jesus have a halo in this picture?** (*Show the children that Jesus has a "natural glow." It's hard to see it in this picture because he's still just a baby. But his glow gets brighter as he gets older.*)

• **Could Mary and Joseph turn the halos off?** (*Yes. But only at night—so the halos wouldn't keep them awake—or while they were in church, where we should never be a distraction. Ever. Ever. Ever.*)

• **Why do Mary and Joseph have to move?** (*An angel came to Joseph in a dream and told him to.*)

• **What would you do if one morning your daddy said, "We're moving because I had a dream"?** (*Make sure they know that good little children don't complain when daddies do silly things.*)

• **What is Joseph looking at in the picture?** (*He's wondering if he left the garage door open back at the house.*)

• **Why does the verse talk about a "flight" into Egypt when there were no planes back then?** (*Jesus knew there would be planes someday. This could explain why he's looking up in the picture.*)

61

REJECTED

- Why do they dress up the donkey like that? (*They use some of the gold from the first wise man; Joseph says it's okay to pimp his ride.*)
- What does the angel in Joseph's dream look like? (*Kind of like a Hooter's waitress.*)
- Is Mary upset about that? (*Oh yeah.*) See Teacher Helps.

TEACHER HELPS

- Point out that in the picture Mary and Joseph aren't looking at each other at all. Explain that sometimes mommies and daddies don't speak to each other when they're mad, and moving is a very stressful time for a family. Also point out that Jesus is looking up to heaven, which is where all good little children look when mommies and daddies fight.

- Point out that Joseph isn't wearing shoes in the picture. Tell the children Joseph probably couldn't find his shoes because they had to leave so quickly. That could have been what Mary and Joseph were fighting about.

CLOSING PRAYER

Traveling God, help us to go where we're told, do what we're told when we get there, and be quiet when we're told to be quiet—especially in church, because we know a quiet church makes you happy. Amen.

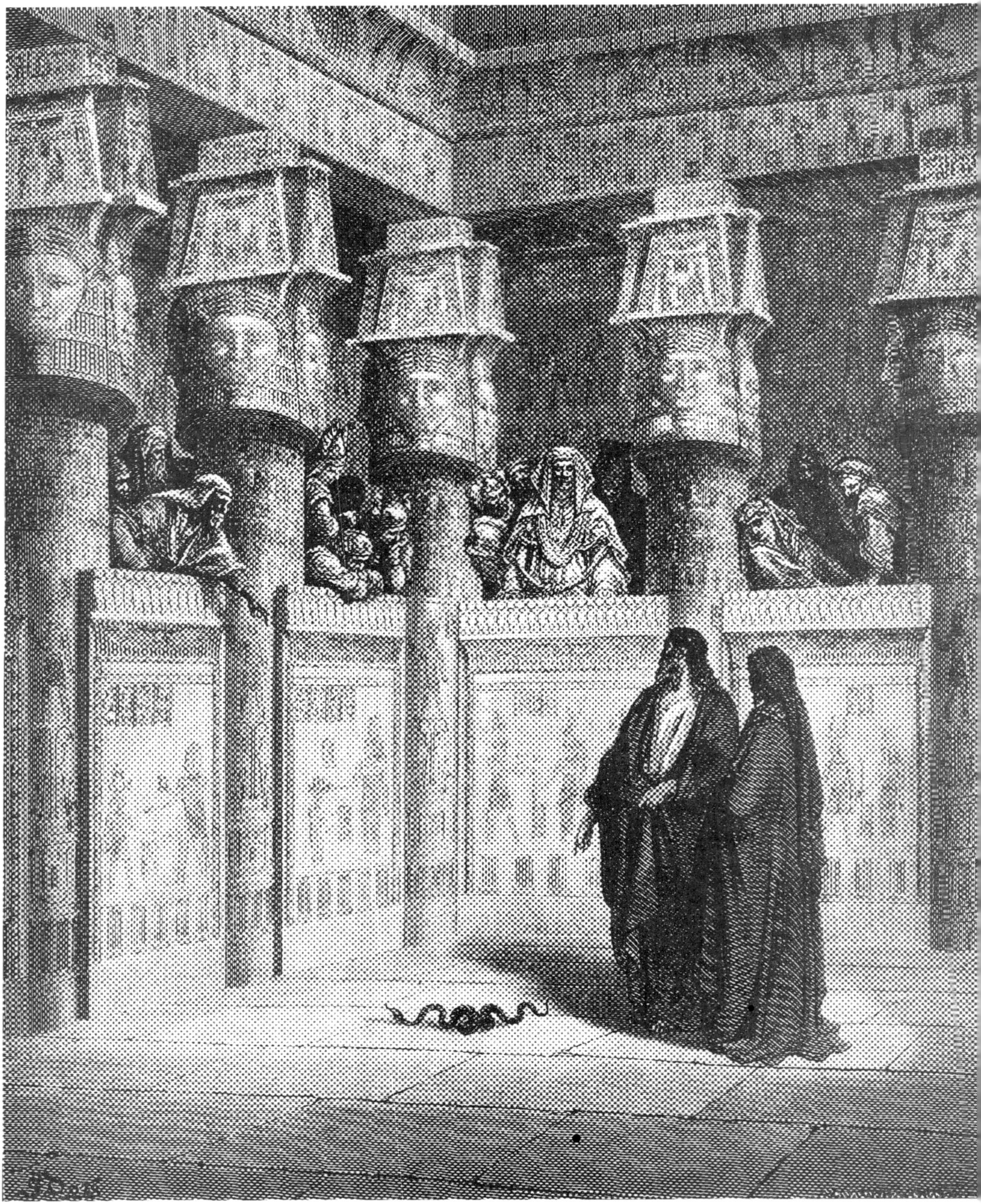

LESSON 15
PHARAOH PHAWCETT MAJORS

REJECTED

SCRIPTURE: Exodus 7:10
MAIN POINT: God doesn't have to like everybody if he doesn't want to.

CHILDREN'S ACTIVITY

Find a live snake from your garden. If snakes frighten you, find a male teacher who isn't a sissy to do this part for you. Have the children go into the church yard and find sticks that look like snakes and bring them into the Sunday school room. Have the children stand in a circle and take turns throwing their sticks on the ground, just like Moses. Tell the children that if they really have enough faith, maybe God will do the same miracle for them. When no one is successful, say something like, **Okay, my turn!** Then quickly toss the real snake into the middle of the circle. Shout—**It's a miracle!** Gather the children back together, catch the snake, and allow the children to pet it before releasing it out the window. (Note: If your snake, for some reason, doesn't survive this activity, explain that it must have been a really old snake, and that God doesn't like snakes anyway because Satan was once a snake.)

DISCUSSION QUESTIONS

• Show the picture to the children and point out that it appears as though a snake is playing a role in our Bible story once more. **What was God's opinion of Pharaoh, since it takes something as evil as a snake to get his attention?** (*Pharaoh was a very bad man.*)

• Show the children the people in the illustration who are sitting in the gallery. Say—**Notice how some look really bored. What do you think happens to the people who don't pay attention when the angel of death flies by?** (*They probably die with all the other people who aren't God's favorites.*)

• **What do you think happens to people who don't pay attention in church or school?** (*They get bitten by snakes.*)

65

REJECTED

- Show the children the picture again and point out that Pharaoh seems to have no reaction at all. **What do you think happens to him?** (*God makes him sad by taking away his son.*)

- **Do you think Moses or his brother, Aaron, could have hidden the snakes in their robes?** (*No! This was a miracle. We don't question miracles.*) If any student answers *yes*, offer to let him hide the snake you brought to class in his clothing and make it look as though he produced the snake.

- **Aren't there some magicians who do tricks with snakes?** (*Yes. But most of them work in Las Vegas, and God's going to burn Sin City to the ground anyway.*)

TEACHING HELPS

- Remind the children that Moses isn't the sharpest tool in the shed, and he has a speech impediment, too. So his brother, Aaron, went along to help. Ask if they know any children with speech impediments, and why it's important not to laugh at these other children—even if they do sound funny when they talk.

- As you talk about the story of Moses, don't forget the part about Passover. This is when the angel of death "passes over" the houses marked with lamb's blood. (Some of the children may have daddies who were passed over for promotions. This is entirely different.)

- Some of the children may bring up the fact that Moses and his people weren't Christians, they were Jewish. Compliment the children who know the difference, but explain that God wanted Moses to stay Jewish so God could bring Moses back during the "transfiguration" story in the New Testament (Matthew 17:1-6).

- Don't forget to tell the children about the part of the story where the Jewish people complain that the journey was taking *tooooooo loooong,* so God made the trip even *longer* for them. Explain to the children why it's important to never complain on long car trips.

CLOSING PRAYER

God, help us to listen better so we don't die when the angel of death flies over our houses when we aren't expecting it. Amen.

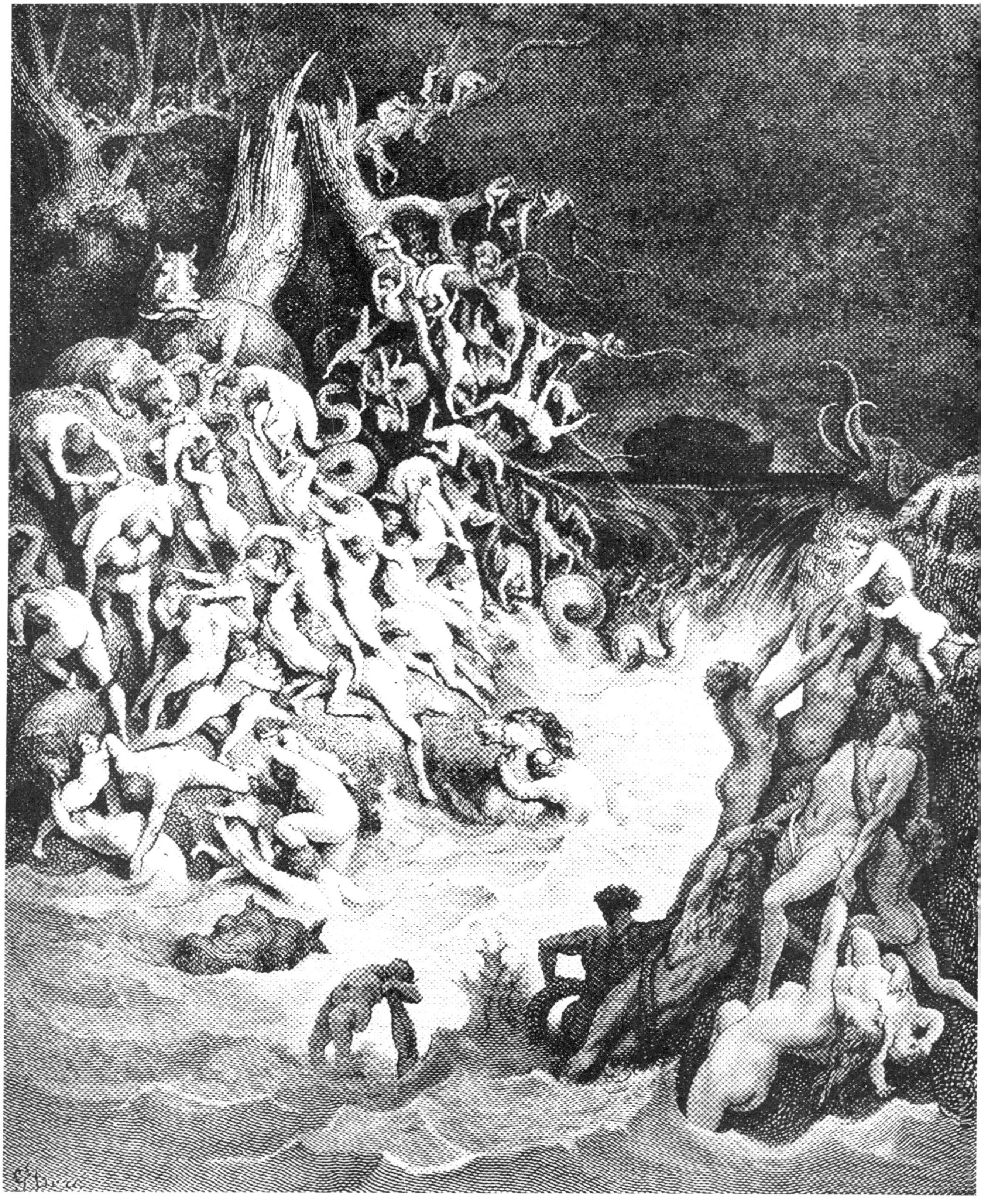

LESSON 16
SWIMMING FOR JESUS

REJECTED

SCRIPTURE: Genesis 7
MAIN POINT: Do what God says, or you might get left behind.

CHILDREN'S ACTIVITY

Fill a large mixing bowl with milk. Now dump several boxes of animal crackers into the bowl. Tell the children they're going "bobbing for God's creatures." The idea is to put one's face in the bowl and select a cracker. Children must then immediately try again and see if they can now catch the same animal. When a child gets two of the same creature, she wins. Tell the children how difficult it must have been for Noah and his family to find all the animals. Especially after it started raining. Emphasize the importance of starting a job early.

You can also teach the children the "Noah Way" song (sung to the melody of "Are You Sleeping?"):

> God told Noah to get some animals
> Noah way! Noah Way!
> Then it started raining because he was complaining
> Noah Way! Noah Way!
>
> Other people tried to come in then
> Go Away! Go Away!
> Friends and neighbors all died, can't we come inside?
> Noah Way! Noah Way!

DISCUSSION QUESTIONS

- **Is God mad at everybody except Noah and his family?** (*Yes. The Bible says God is very disappointed.*)

- **Is he mad at the children and the puppies, too?** (*Yes. The children were bad. If they'd been good, then God would have let them on the ark, too. And Noah already had two dogs, so he didn't need any puppies.*)

REJECTED

- **Were all the people on earth naked then, just like in the picture?** (*Everybody except Noah and his family; that's partly why God was so mad.*)

- **Would God ever do that again?** (*God promises to never cover the earth with water again, but there aren't any guarantees against fire or ice or mud or other disasters.*)

- **What do Noah and his family do with all the animal droppings?** (*He saves them for fertilizer in the new world.*)

- **Does Noah really have polar bears on the ark? How did he get them?** (*Yes. Noah has two of everything. Most likely either God brought the polar bears to Noah, or Noah picked them up when they floated by on an iceberg.*)

- **What about sharks?** (*The sharks just swam beside the ark and ate the pesky flood survivors.*)

TEACHER HELPS

- The title of this lesson is "Swimming for Jesus." Make sure the children know that if Jesus had come to earth at the time of the flood, then the saved people would have been on the ark, too. But they all went to hell instead.

- Show the picture to the children and ask if they see any unusual animals. There are several in the picture that we don't see today. This proves that extinction is part of God's overall plan. In other words, people who get upset about losing the spotted owl forever are going against what God wants.

- If you start hearing too many questions like, "But what about the kitty cats?" you can point to the picture of the people clinging to the rocks and say, "These children asked a lot of questions, too — and look what happened to them!"

CLOSING PRAYER

God, please don't cover the earth with water ever again. Some of us don't know how to swim yet. Amen.

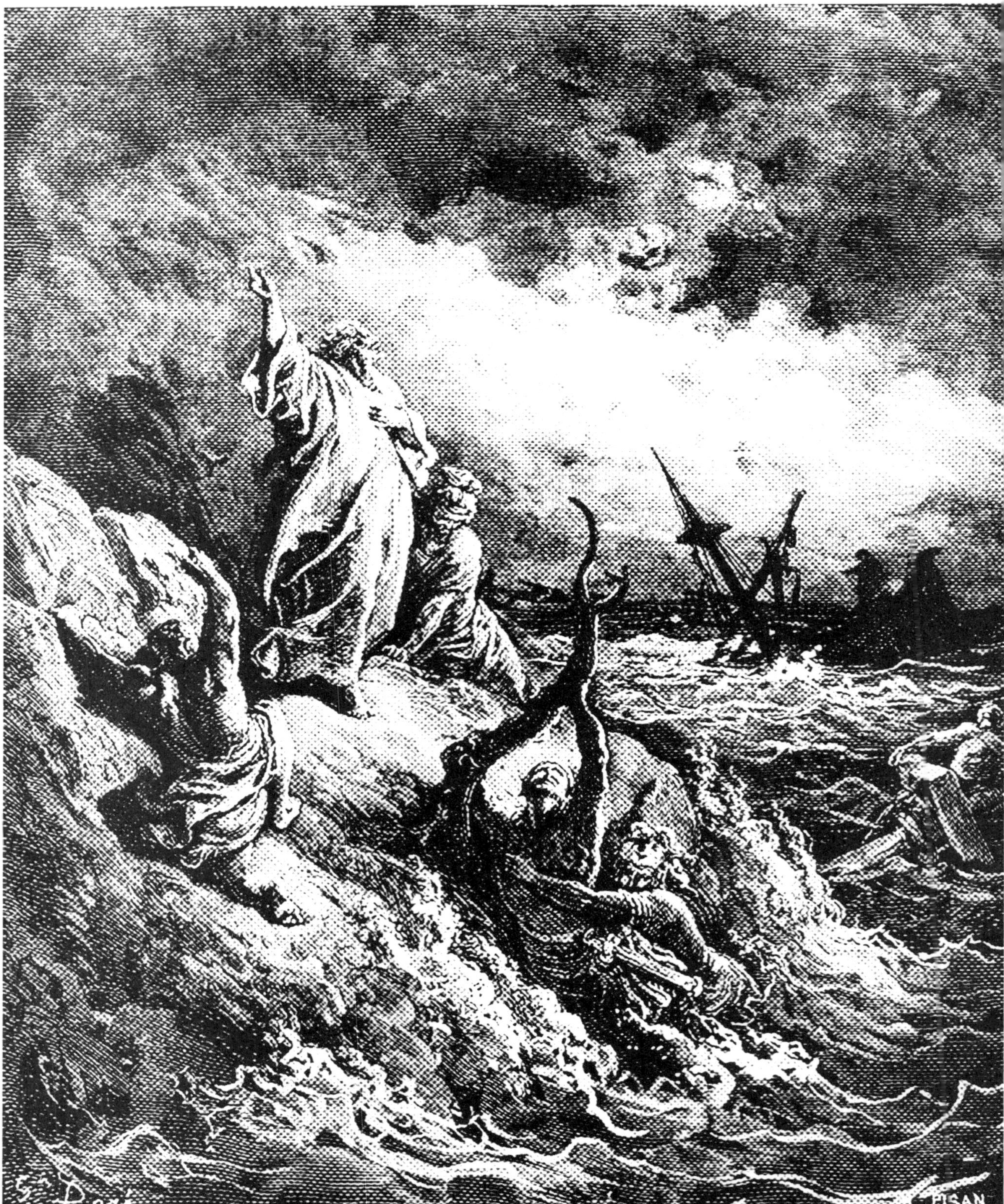

LESSON 17

REJECTED

IN DEEP SHIP

SCRIPTURE: Acts 27:3-44
MAIN POINT: TV weather forecasters are stupid.

CHILDREN'S ACTIVITY

Before class begins, fill up some balloons with water. Once the children are seated for class, teach them this little "Rain Game" rhyme:

> Paul said it was going to rain
> But his speech was spoken in vain
> The sailors ignored the words from his lips
> Then God reached down and sank their ship
> How many sailors nearly drown? 1...2...3...4...

This game is similar to Duck, Duck, Goose. Have the children sit in a circle. Select one child to walk around the circle carrying a water balloon. He should carefully tap the other children on their heads with the balloon while the whole group recites the rhyme they just learned. The child with the balloon must bust the balloon over another child's head before the group reaches the number 10. The soaked child then chases the "runner" around the circle and back to his own seat. If she tags the runner, she may sit back down. Then the first child repeats the process using a new water balloon.

DISCUSSION QUESTIONS

• Read the Scripture passage and point out how many times the men on the boat don't listen to Paul's advice. Ask the children if they've ever heard of someone staying behind when the TV weatherman says to leave town.

• Ask them if they've ever heard of someone being struck by lightning. Explain that sometimes people get struck by God's lightning when they're bad, and sometimes they get struck by lightning because they were stupid and went outside during a thunderstorm.

REJECTED

- **Who is your local weather forecaster? Have you ever watched her talk about the weather while standing outside in a hurricane?**
- **Why didn't the sailors listen to Paul?** (*They don't know Paul's an expert in meteorology.*)
- **What happens to all the stuff the sailors throw overboard?** (*Some of it washes up on shore. Some sinks to the bottom. Some of it is now available on eBay.*)
- **If an angel of God told Paul that everything was going to be okay, why didn't the angel just stop the storm from coming in the first place?** (*Only Jesus can do that.*)
- **If someone said an avalanche was about to occur, what kind of people would leave their houses and go to the bottom of the hill to watch?** (*Stupid people.*)
- **Are all of God's top people (disciples, apostles, prophets, and so on) able to predict the weather?** (*No. But some of them could talk to animals.*)
- **Do all of God's followers get superpowers?** (*Usually, yes. But you have to love God very, very, very much.*)

TEACHER HELPS

- Show the picture to the children and ask them to count the survivors. (*Answer: Seven*) Ask the kids if they've ever heard of a TV show called *Gilligan's Island*.
- Point out that only Paul seems "high and dry," but if the "wet" children really loved God, they'd still be dry, too.

CLOSING PRAYER

God, keep us from being stupid. Don't make us into weather forecasters. Amen.

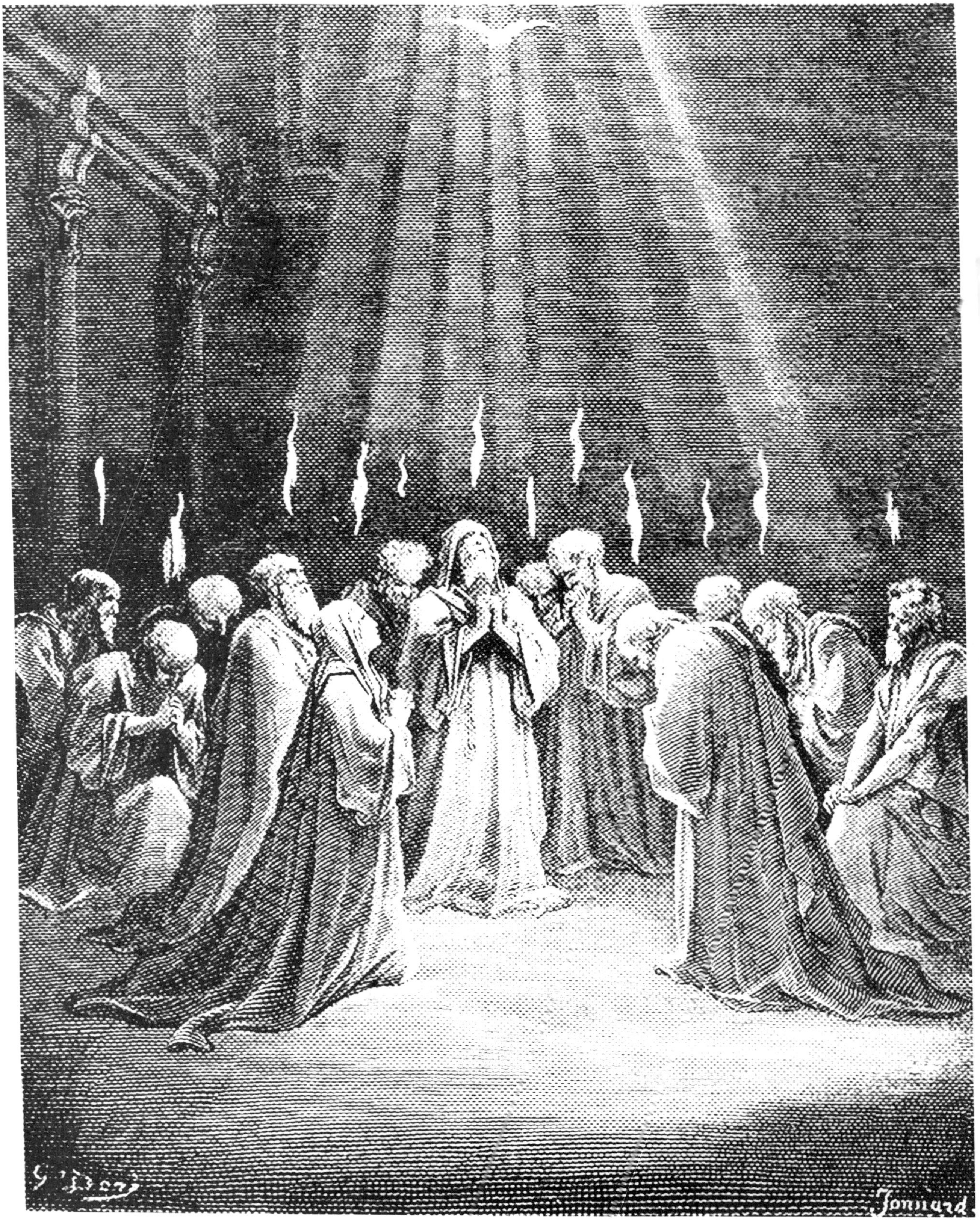
G. Doré
Jonnard

LESSON 18 ~~REJECTED~~
IT'S A BOY (*OR* THE BIRTH OF THE CHURCH)

SCRIPTURE: Acts 2:1-21
MAIN POINT: Never look up when you're supposed to be praying.

CHILDREN'S ACTIVITY

Have the children assume the "praying position" (kneeling with their hands folded in front of them). Remind the children that this is how God hears us best. Have an assistant stand to the side with a Super Soaker loaded and ready. Tell the children they're going to pray, and should any of them look up before you say to, they'll get spritzed in the back of the head—just like the Holy Spirit did to the disciples. Give a prize to the child who "prays" the longest.

Pentecost is often referred to as "the birth of the church," so you could also try hosting a birthday party for the church. If you plan these sessions in advance (and if you truly love Jesus, you always plan things in advance), tell the children to get ready for a birthday party during the next class time. Check your craft cupboard, make a list of any supplies you need, and send a note home with your students that explains the party and includes a list of suggested supplies the parents could donate that would make great gifts for the party.

DISCUSSION QUESTIONS

- **Why are all the disciples gathered in one place?** (*To replace Judas.*)

- **What happens to Judas?** (*He buys a field with his 30 pieces of silver, and then his bowels explode.*)

- **Doesn't he hang himself?** (*He does. He hangs himself in a field, and then his bowels explode.*)

- **Why don't the disciples let Mary become one of the disciples?** (*Mary's busy cleaning the upper room.*)

REJECTED

- **The Scripture says everyone thought the disciples were drunk. But Peter says they aren't drunk because it's only nine in the morning. Does that mean the disciples drank wine later in the day?** (*Just the Episcopalian disciples.*)
- **The Methodist disciples didn't drink?** (*Not in front of each other.*)
- **Is there ever a "good" time to be drunk?** (*Ask me after class.*)
- **The Bible says the disciples draw straws to replace Judas; isn't that like gambling?** (*No. It didn't happen in Las Vegas.*)
- **What happened to the man called Justus?** (*He joined the finance committee and helped raise money for the disciples' new Family Life Center.*) Don't forget to ask the children if they have any spare change.
- **The Bible says people from other nations heard the disciples speaking in their own languages. How did they do that?** (*Jesus is magic.*)

TEACHER HELPS

- One of your students may point out that in the picture it looks as though the Holy Spirit was "dropping" on everyone, not just those looking up from their prayers. Tell the children that the other disciples (yes, even the woman) were probably letting their minds wander to thoughts about what they were going to have for lunch after church. (Note: It looks as though the disciple third from the left has been spared a "gift" from the dove.)

CLOSING PRAYER

God, thank you for creating the church. Help us keep focused so that the dove of the Holy Spirit doesn't poop on our heads. Amen.

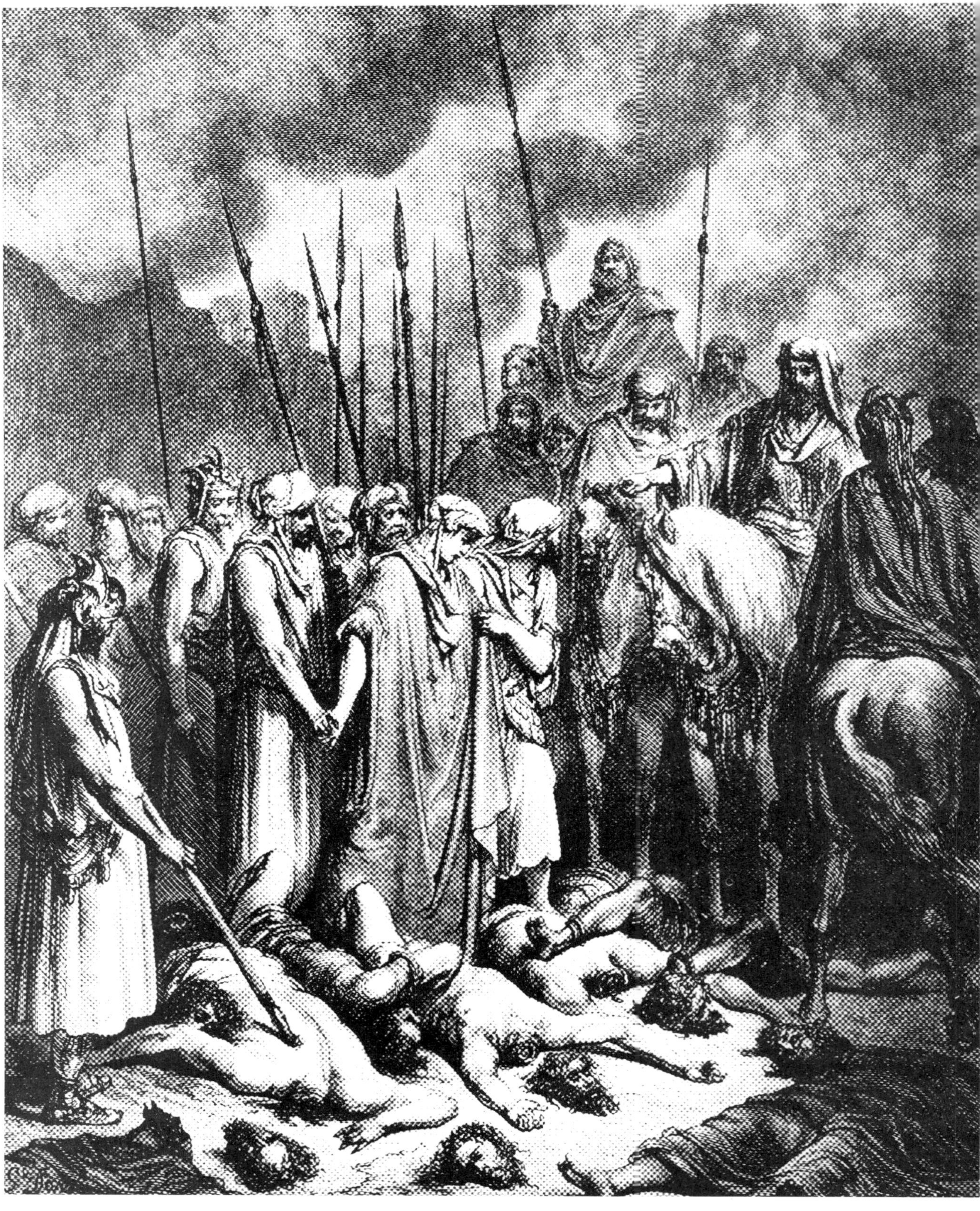

LESSON 19
NNNNNNEXT!

REJECTED

SCRIPTURE: Joshua 2:1-21; 6:21-25
MAIN POINT: God won't hold it against you if you don't hold "it" against someone else.

CHILDREN'S ACTIVITY

Take your children to the roof of the church. Talk about how exciting it must have been for two of Joshua's spies to be on top of the wall surrounding Jericho, where Rahab's apartment was located. Read to them how Rahab used a rope to lower them out her window and down to the ground. Now hang a rope down from the church roof and play "Let's Pretend," allowing the children to climb down the rope—all the way to the ground. (Note: If you're working with children under seven years old, simply tie the rope around their waists and lower them to the ground one by one. Have your teaching partner stand on the ground below, just in case there's an emergency.)

DISCUSSION QUESTIONS

Note: This is an important subject to talk about with your children, but you don't want to open certain doors that are best left closed at their age. So when discussing what Rahab does for a living, simply refer to her as "a really, really good date."[1]

• **Who is Rahab?** (*Rahab lives in Jericho; she's a really, really good date.*)

• **Why are Joshua's spies hiding on Rahab's roof?** (*To tell Rahab that God loves her.*)

• **Does everyone in Jericho love Rahab?** (*Pretty much.*)

• **Why does Rahab save Joshua's spies?** (*Because she wants to save her family and their asses.*)

---

[1] *The phrase "really, really good date" was provided by Craig McNair Wilson.*

REJECTED

- It's a big city; how do the soldiers know where Rahab lives, and that she might be the one hiding the strangers? (*Rahab was a really, really good date.*)
- Was Rahab especially good at keeping secrets? (*Most of them.*)
- Rahab is the mother of Boaz, who's the grandfather of Jesse, who's King David's daddy. The Bible says Jesus was also part of David's family tree. Ask the children if they know their own family trees. Are there any "really, really good dates" in their family histories?
- Is the man at the back of the picture sitting on a horse, or is he just really tall like Goliath? (*He's probably sitting on a horse or on a friend's shoulders. There are no giants around until David discovers them many years later.*)

TEACHER HELPS

- Show the children the picture of Joshua sparing Rahab and her family. Tell them that Rahab may have deserved to be "speared" instead of "spared" because of her reputation. Tell the girls how important it is for them to have good reputations when they get older.

- Point out the variety of heads on the ground and how Rahab seems to be looking at them as though she's searching for her old boyfriends.

- Point out how Rahab is holding hands with someone. Explain that he's probably one of Joshua's spies. Rahab becomes good friends with him while he was hiding on her roof. Tell the children that holding hands is as far as Rahab would "go" now that she's saved—that is, until she married that spy. Then share with the class that holding hands is as far as all good girls should go, too, or else they might be called "Rahabs."

CLOSING PRAYER

God, help us to always keep a good reputation so we don't get beheaded when you return. Amen.

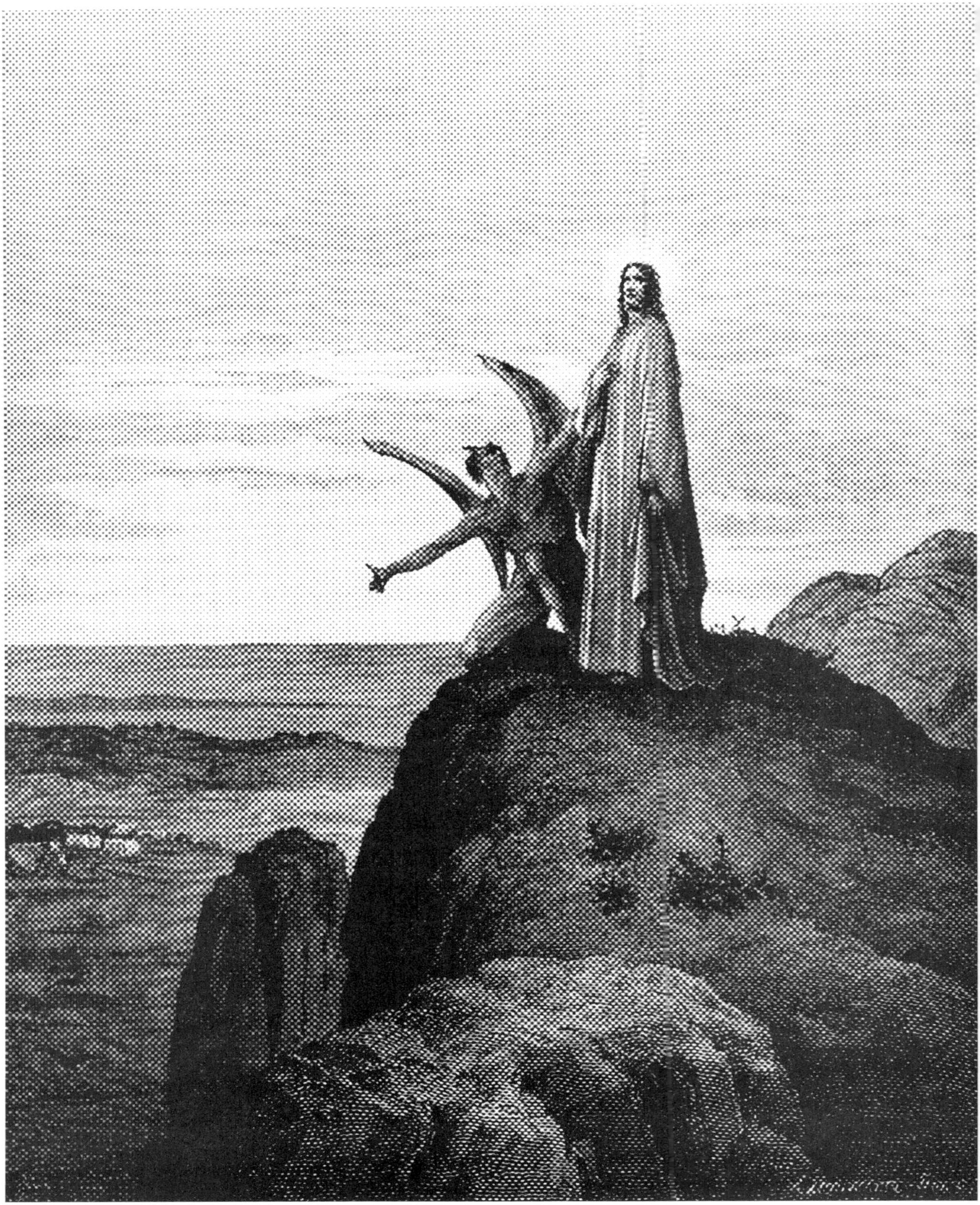

LESSON 20
THE HILLS ARE ALIIIIIIIIIVVVVVVVE

REJECTED

SCRIPTURE: Joshua 7:1-25
MAIN POINT: Jesus didn't succumb to temptation or musical theater.

CHILDREN'S ACTIVITY

Ahead of time, collect at least a dozen mousetraps so you can make a nice, long trail. Then buy a large bag of peanut butter M&Ms for bait. First, get one of the children to volunteer to walk the trail blindfolded...

> THE CREATORS OF REJECTED SUNDAY SCHOOL LESSONS WOULD LIKE TO TAKE THIS OPPORTUNITY TO APOLOGIZE TO ALL THE WONDERFUL PEOPLE WHO'VE VOLUNTEERED THEIR TIME AND TALENTS TO TEACH THE LOVE OF GOD TO THE CHILDREN IN YOUR CONGREGATIONS. JUST BECAUSE YOU MAY (OR MAY NOT) HAVE CHUCKLED, GIGGLED, TITTERED, GUFFAWED, OR LAUGHED OUT LOUD, THAT DOESN'T MAKE YOU A BAD PERSON. WE DO NOT NOW—NOR HAVE WE EVER—ENDORSED THE HARMING OF CHILDREN WITH MOUSETRAPS (OR ANY OTHER DEVICES). PLEASE REMEMBER: THIS BOOK IS A JOKE!

...and be prepared with extra bandages.

DISCUSSION QUESTIONS

• **Is Jesus wearing a cape in the picture?** (*No. But Jesus does wear a big robe that can be used as a parachute, just as a precaution.*)

• **The Bible says the devil tells Jesus to turn stones into bread. But why wouldn't the devil tempt Jesus with something better—like ice cream or cookies?** (*Jesus had just eaten a big breakfast.*)

• **Is the devil really auditioning for Jesus?** (*Yes. The devil thought musical theater was a pretty good idea. He brought it up again after Jesus returned to heaven and just wouldn't let it go.*)

• **What song does the devil sing?** (*Probably something from* The Sound of Music.)

REJECTED

- Why isn't the devil wearing pants? (*The devil never wears pants; that's why we should never be naked except when we're bathing.*)

- How come Jesus always has that light around his head? (*Because he's holy.*)

- Does he ever use it as a night-light? (*No. Only people who don't really trust Jesus use baby night-lights.*)

- Could Jesus turn off his light in church or school? (*Yes. But then people wouldn't know who he was, and that was why he was here on earth.*)

- Why does the devil have wings? I thought only angels have wings! (*The devil's wings are made of black leather—a tool of the devil if there ever was one—not the white feathers worn by God's real angels. The devil uses his wings to fan the flames of sin in our hearts.*)

TEACHER HELPS

- Point out how Jesus isn't even looking at the devil or the city—instead, he seems to be looking at *you*. Explain to the children that Jesus is always watching them. He watches what they do and where they go, and he knows what they're thinking—all the time.

- Point out that the devil is also called *Satan,* and that Satan tries to sneak into our lives all the time. See if the children can rearrange the letters in Satan's name to discover a place were Satan "sneaks in." (Here's a hint: S-A-_-T-A.)

CLOSING PRAYER

Special God, keep us from wanting and thinking bad things. Bless our teachers who can show us what the bad things are. Amen.

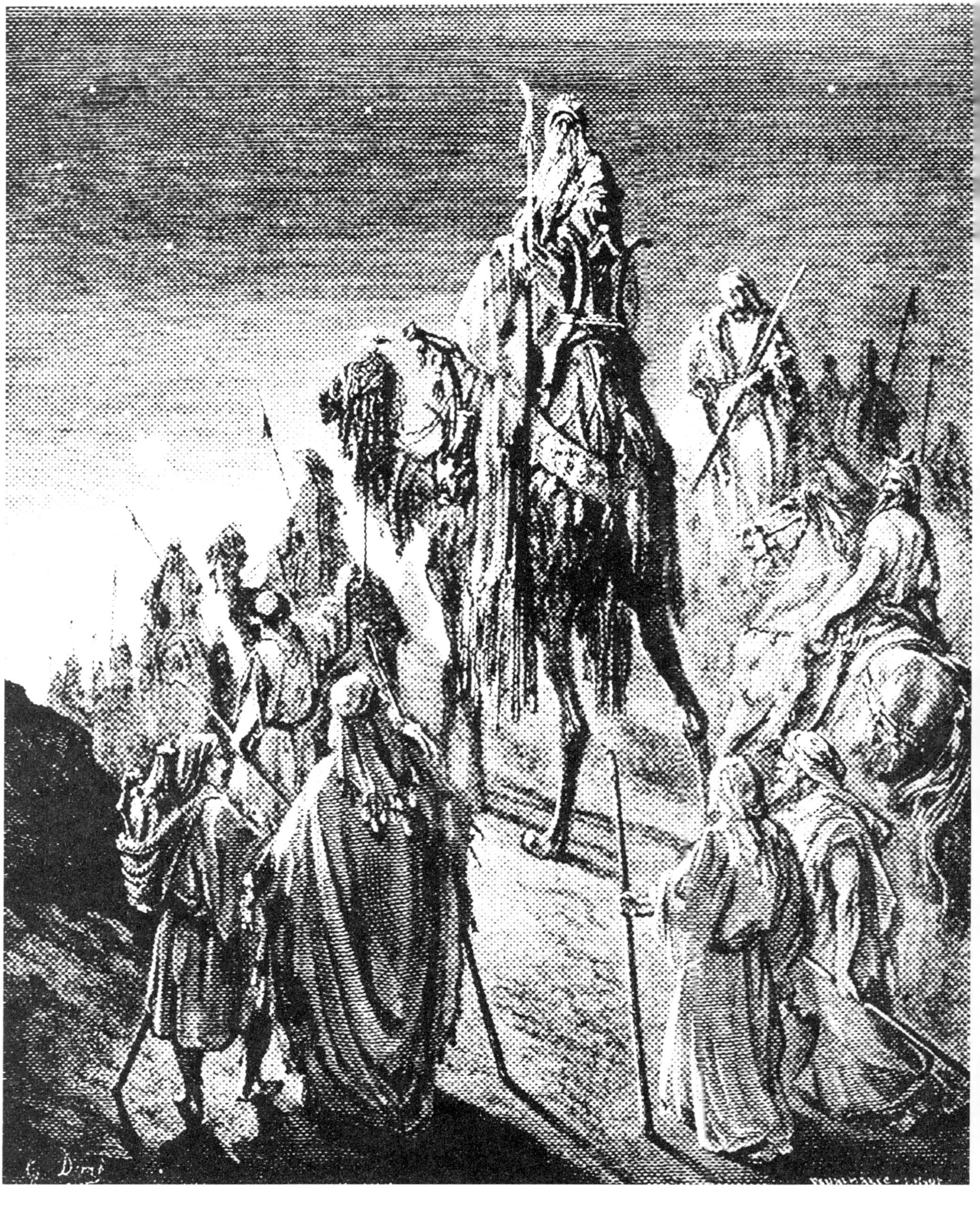

LESSON 21
PIMP MY RIDE

REJECTED

SCRIPTURE: Matthew 2:1-12
MAIN POINT: God wants us to be stylin'.

CHILDREN'S ACTIVITY

Show the picture to the children and point out the wise men's decked-out camels. Explain that people in Jesus' time who were held in high regard got to travel first class. Then pass out a variety of stickers and craft supplies and tell the children they're going to show the senior pastor how much they appreciate him. After several minutes of making paper chains and aluminum foil stars, quietly sneak out to the senior pastor's car and decorate it. If it's raining or if you live in a windy area, you might want to use duct tape to secure the decorations.

DISCUSSION QUESTIONS

• **Was following a star a very "wise" thing to do? Wouldn't a street map have been more helpful?** (*Probably yes. But God tested the wise men's faith to see if they could make the journey with just the star.*)

• **Who are all the other people in the picture?** (*Probably the wise men's servants, plus some townsfolk on their way to Bethlehem to get counted in the census.*)

• **Why don't they have camels?** (*Because they're poor, like Jesus.*)

• **The wise men bring gold, frankincense, and myrrh. Why don't they bring the baby Jesus some toys?** (*Because they know Jesus is going to die for their sins, so they don't want him to get too attached to things here on earth.*)

TEACHER HELPS

• Point out to the children that one of the wise men in the picture seems to be looking back at them. Say—**Could he be asking, "Where's *your* gift?"**

REJECTED

- There's someone in the foreground on the left side of the picture who looks as though he's carrying a large jar, probably full of myrrh or frankincense. Explain to the children that rich people usually traveled with an "entourage," and they rarely had to carry their own stuff.

CLOSING PRAYER

God, help us to be faithful and to remember that the only gifts Jesus really wants are our souls. Amen.

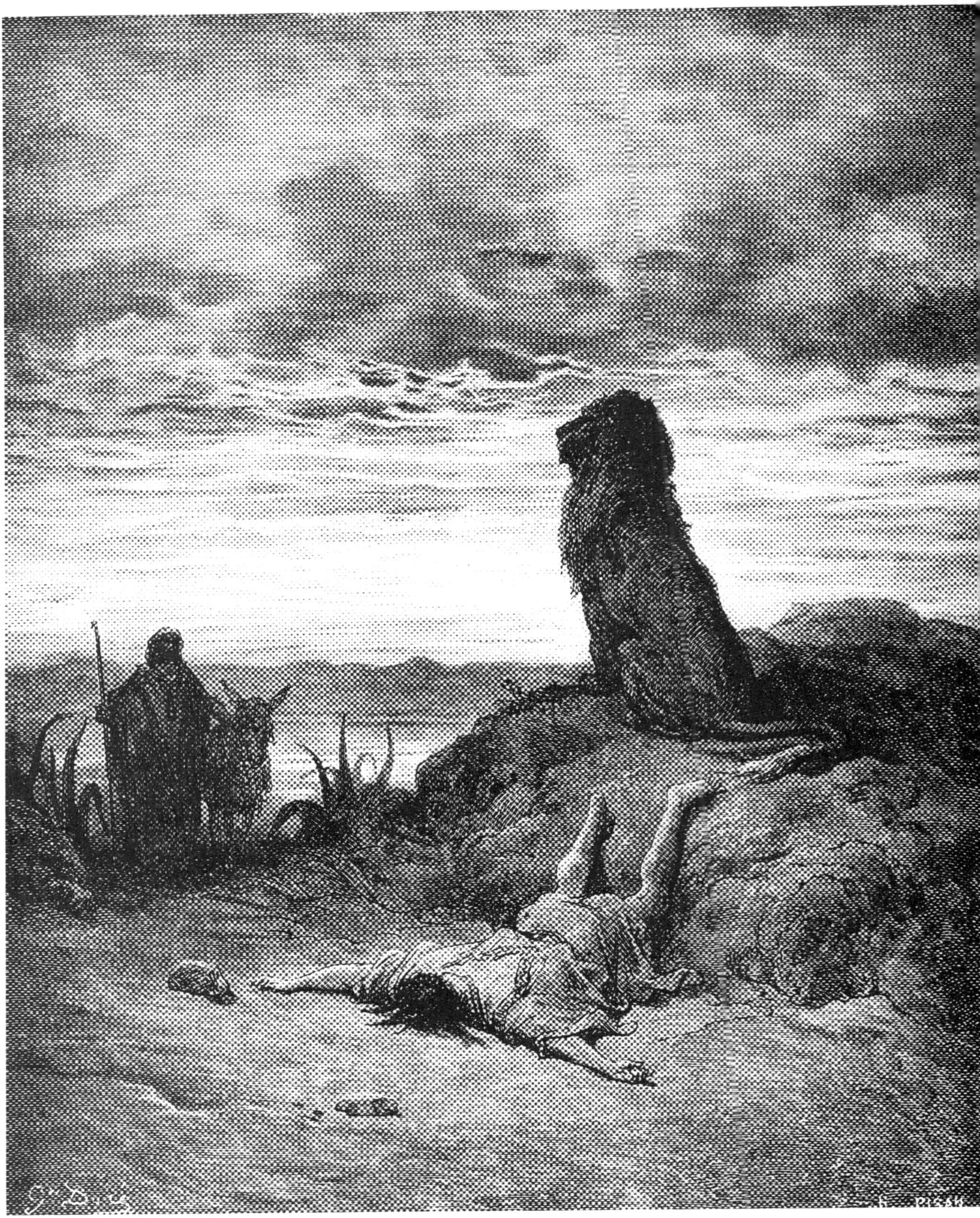

LESSON 22
CAN YOU HEAR ME *NOW?*

REJECTED

SCRIPTURE: 1 Kings 13:11-26
MAIN POINT: Be careful who you listen to.

CHILDREN'S ACTIVITY

Cover the table in your Sunday school room with a brightly colored tablecloth. Then arrange plates full of Twinkies, Krispy Kremes, Oreos, Peanut Butter Cups, and M&Ms on the table. Before the children arrive, count how many items are on each plate, and make a note of it for later on in the lesson.

Read the Scripture passage to the children. Now tell them they're going to pretend to be the holy men they just heard about in the story. Seat the children around the table and tell them God said they're not to eat anything. Turn your back to the children so you can write a Bible verse on the board, but listen closely so you'll know if any children make a move for the food. More than likely, at least one will try to sneak a treat. If you discover something is missing from a plate, ask the children who took it. If no one answers, ask the children to help God by pointing to the person who stole the treat. (Someone is always willing to tattle.) Then point at the disobedient child and—in your best "exorcist" voice—shout, "You disobeyed God! For that you are going to die far from home!" Grab the child and shoo him out of the room for the remainder of the session.

DISCUSSION QUESTIONS

• **Why does God send a lion to kill the holy man?** (*Because the man listens to someone else instead of God.*)

• **God sure seems to like working with lions, huh?** (*Yes, God often uses lions because penguins aren't very intimidating.*)

• **Why does the old prophet lie to the holy man?** (*He wanted the holy man's donkey.*)

REJECTED

- **How is the holy man supposed to know it isn't good to eat the food?** (*He should have only listened to God.*)

- **How are we supposed to know if God is talking to us?** (*You'll know; but if you aren't sure, why risk it?*)

- **Aren't ministers supposed to tell us what God says? Isn't that their job?** (*Yes. But most ministers don't want our stuff.*)

- **Who are we supposed to obey if we don't hear God?** (*Mommies, daddies, preachers, Sunday school teachers, and regular school teachers—as long as they don't say anything bad about the Bible.*)

- **Do you think the lion in the picture looks like Aslan from the Narnia books?** (*This is a trick question because the Narnia books are fiction, and the Bible is true—so it isn't even close to the same lion!*)

TEACHER HELPS

- Point out that we can't see the holy man's face in the picture. That's probably because God's lion ate it. Since they didn't have crime scene investigators back then and because the Bible never gives the holy man's name, we'll never ever know who he was.

- Point out that the lion doesn't eat the man or the donkey. In the picture he's just standing there like the statues you see in front of some libraries. Remind the children that libraries are full of books that aren't the Bible—books that have lots of bad information in them. That's why God put lion statues in front of libraries.

- Point out that the old prophet, even though he works for God, tells a lie to the holy man. Ask the children—**Do you think it's okay for preachers to tell lies?** (Gather the children's opinions and keep a list.)

CLOSING PRAYER

God, help us to listen to you and obey you so you don't send wild animals to eat our faces. Amen.

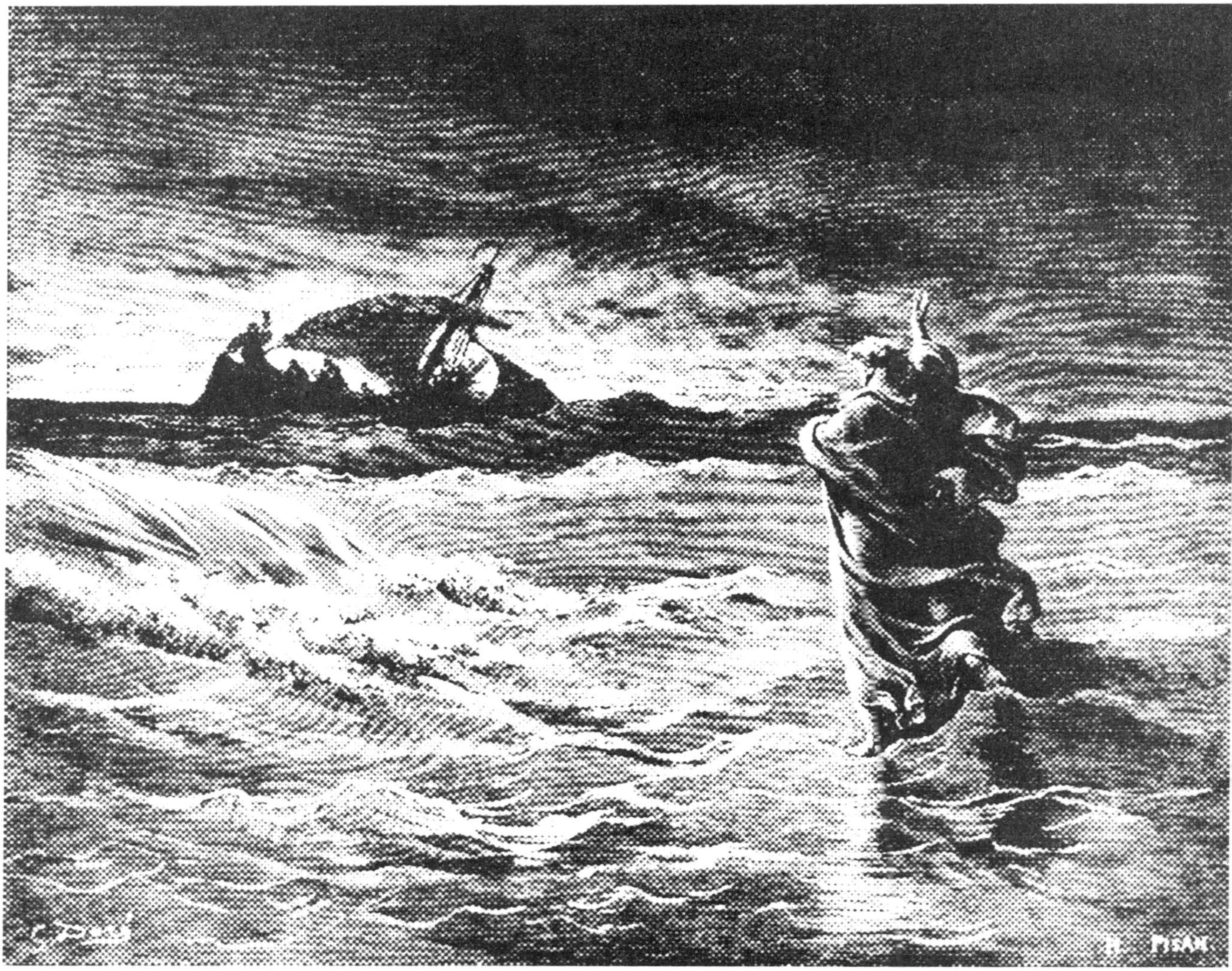

LESSON 23
GETTING IN OVER YOUR HEAD

SCRIPTURE: Matthew 14:22-31
MAIN POINT: Just because your friends do stupid things doesn't mean you have to.

CHILDREN'S ACTIVITY

Give each of the children a water balloon to hold in both hands. Tell them they must hold the water in the same shape as the balloon—or something really bad might happen to their moms or dads. Then go around the room with a pin and pop each balloon.

DISCUSSION QUESTIONS

- What happens when Peter tries to get out of the boat? (*He almost sinks.*)
- Does the Bible say anything about the other disciples trying to stop Peter's stupid behavior? (*No. Maybe they want him to learn a lesson the hard way, or maybe they aren't really his friends.*)
- Who's your best friend? (*Jesus.*)
- If one of your friends at school does something stupid, like taking drugs, and they want you to do it, too…and you do… what does that make you? (*Stupid.*)
- What happens when we sometimes feel as though we're more important than Jesus? (*We almost sink.*)
- Why would Jesus ask us to step onto the water and then almost let us drown? (*To test our faith.*)
- What should Peter have done? (*He should have stayed in the boat and believed that Jesus was the Son of God because Jesus told him so.*)

TEACHER HELPS

- Children might feel bad if they can't do the task correctly. Make sure you tell them that you forgive them—and so does Jesus.

REJECTED

- Show the children the picture of Jesus walking on the water. Point out that we only see Jesus doing this—no one else. Remind the children they're not Jesus.

- Point out that Jesus isn't really walking "on" the water; the picture clearly shows Jesus *above* the water. Make sure the children know that Jesus never got his feet dirty, either, and that he's above us all.

CLOSING PRAYER

God, forgive us when we do stupid things because our friends tell us to. Only your Son Jesus can do miracles. Amen.

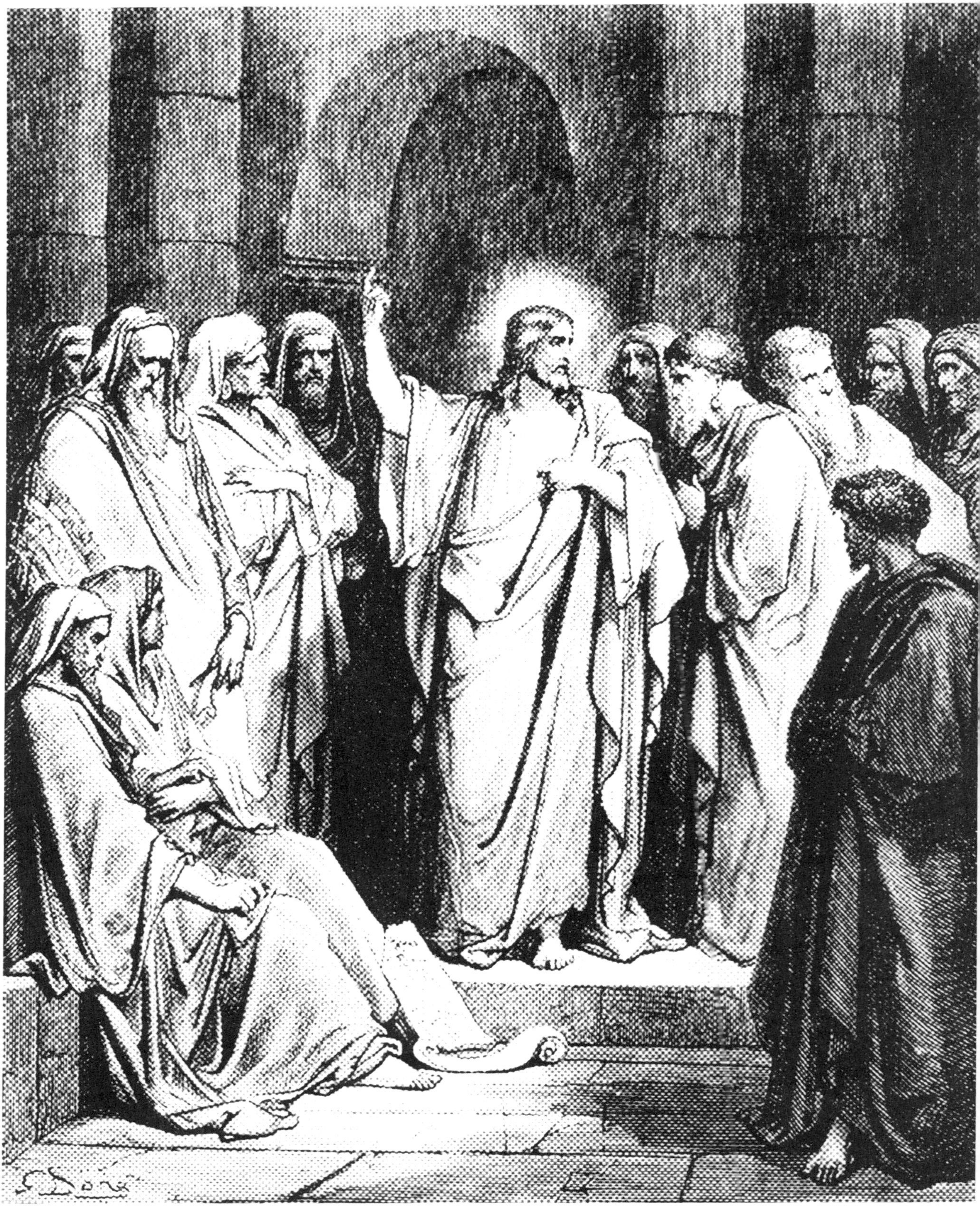

LESSON 24
HE CAN FLY!

REJECTED

SCRIPTURE: Luke 4:22-30
MAIN POINT: Not everybody wants to hear what you have to say.

CHILDREN'S ACTIVITY

Does your church have access to the roof? If so, take your children up there and let them play a game of tag. Before they begin the game, explain that in today's Bible story the crowd in the synagogue chased Jesus around, but they couldn't catch him. (Caution: be sure you tell the children they can't fly like Jesus, so they must not try to copy him.)

Another idea is to make a list of words or terms that anger people in your church, such as *capital campaign*, *volunteer*, *youth minister*, and *biblically sound*. Tell the children that the next time they attend big people's church on a Sunday morning, they should jump up and scream those words when no one is expecting them to. (See? These words really *do* make people angry!)

101

DISCUSSION QUESTIONS

• **The Bible says the people in Jesus' church were so angry with him they even tried to throw him off a cliff. Did Jesus fly like Superman, or did he just stop himself from falling right before he hit the ground?** (*He probably just stopped before he hit the ground. Jesus isn't a show off.*)

• **How come Peter Pan needed pixie dust to fly?** (*Peter Pan got his "dust" from Tinker Bell; Jesus was celibate.*)

• **What does *celibate* mean?** (*Tell your mommy she has celibate on the back of her legs, and your daddy will think you are very funny.*)

• **In the picture what's that paper lying on the ground near Jesus' feet?** (*It's a scroll. That's what people used to read in church before we had the New Testament.*)

REJECTED

• **Are the men mad because Jesus dropped it on the ground?** (*Jesus didn't really drop it. One of the other men probably pushed it off with his foot and blamed Jesus. In any case, it doesn't matter now because we have the "real" Bible in the New Testament.*)

• **How come there are no women in the temple?** (*There are women in the temple. They're just working hard in the kitchen and making snacks for after the service.*)

• **How come the man on the left is sticking his foot out like that?** (*He's hoping to trip Jesus and laugh at him when he falls down.*)

• **How come the man who's trying to trip Jesus has a goatee?** (*Because he's actually Satan. Only Satan and youth ministers have goatees.*)

• **Could Jesus really be saying he is the Son of God?** (*Maybe. He could also be showing them a booger on his finger. Jesus made boogers that healed people.*)

• **Why does the man on the left look sad?** (*Jesus told him he's too old to fly.*)

TEACHER HELPS

• Point out how much brighter Jesus' "glow" is now that he's grown up.

• Point out the faces of the men in the synagogue and how angry they look. Ask the children if there are words they use that might make God angry. Ask them where they learned these words. (Keep a list of their offensive words and refer to it the next time you need volunteers for a fundraiser.)

• Look at the picture again. See how Jesus is pointing to himself and pointing up at the sky? He's telling the men he can fly.

CLOSING PRAYER

God, help us remember that we can't fly until we die and become angels. That will be really, really fun to do some day. But not right now. Amen.

Jesus didn't promise to solve all our problems in this life. But he did say he'd be with us through it all. Steve Case's compilation of gritty, real-to-life stories on relevant topics such as integrity, love, family, and faith will make your lessons come to life. Each study is organized by category and topic for easy use.

The Youth Worker's Big Book of Case Studies
Not Quite a Million Stories That Beg Discussion
Steven Case
RETAIL $17.99
ISBN 0-310-25562-7

visit www.youthspecialties.com/store
or your local Christian bookstore

youth specialties

The first in an exciting new Bible study series from Youth Specialties, *Studies on the Go: John* is a quick, pick-up-and-use Bible study that doesn't skimp on depth. You won't need to rewrite questions or reconfigure anything because author (and small group guru) Laurie Polich has made sure every question is appropriate for students. The 30 studies inside will engage your group with open-ended questions and practical applications from the spiritual wisdom of John's Gospel.

Studies on the Go: John
Laurie Polich
RETAIL $8.99
ISBN 0-310-27200-9

visit www.youthspecialties.com/store
or your local Christian bookstore

youth specialties

With more than 100 new ideas added, *Ideas Library on CD-ROM 4.0* lets you search from nearly 4,000 ideas to find the perfect one for your next meeting. You'll find games, icebreakers, Bible lessons, scripts, worship services, and so much more! It's easy to search, print, and use—so you'll have plenty of time to just be with students.

Ideas Library on CD-ROM 4.0
The Most Complete and Practical Ideas on the Planet
Youth Specialties
RETAIL $129.99
ISBN 0-310-25758-1

visit www.youthspecialties.com/store
or your local Christian bookstore

youth specialties

TalkSheets are convenient, effective one-page reproducible handouts with intriguing questions that will get churched kids and unchurched kids alike talking and thinking about the Bible—and how its principles affect their daily lives.

Use TalkSheets to launch your own lesson—or use them as stand-alone Bible studies. Each TalkSheet comes with detailed information and suggestions for discussion leaders, including: Bible references, Internet resources, further group exploration, and activities to pursue during and after the meeting. Perfect for youth meetings, small groups and cell groups, Sunday school, and camps and retreats.

Provocative questions about what the Bible says concerning values and behavior, music videos, marriage, loneliness, Christian social action, and more.

High School Talksheets—Updated!
David Lynn
RETAIL $14.99
ISBN 0-310-23852-8

Get your middle schoolers talking about sin, fears, parents, integrity, and more. These TalkSheets, based on Psalms and Proverbs, will get you students talking about the things that matter.

Junior High & Middle School Talksheets: Psalms and Proverbs—Updated!
Rick Bundschuh
RETAIL $14.99
ISBN 0-310-23851-X

This collection of 50 discussion starters for high schoolers contain a high-interest, topical mix--parents, spiritual stamina, tragedies and suffering, purpose in life, unhealthy friendships, the role of women, and Christian unity--that will keep high schoolers talking at your meetings.

High School Talksheets: Psalms and Proverbs—Updated!
Rick Bundschuh
RETAIL $14.99
ISBN 0-310-23853-6

Add 50 more great questions to your library! These will get high schoolers discovering new perspectives on what the Bible says about the future, cheating, family life, problem solving, and so much more.

More High School Talksheets—Updated!
David Lynn
RETAIL $14.99
ISBN 0-310-23854-4

Get your junior highers talking to each other and defending their points of view by choosing from 50 annotated topics such as loneliness, prayer, world hunger, wisdom, and much, much more.

Junior High & Middle School Talksheets—Updated!
David Lynn
RETAIL $14.99
ISBN 0-310-23855-2

Add a cache of 50 more reproducible pages of lesson-launching topics for junior highers! Subjects include spiritual growth, death, the environment, war, biblical doctrine, and much more.

More Junior High & Middle School Talksheets—Updated!
David Lynn
RETAIL $14.99
ISBN 0-310-23856-0

youth specialties

visit www.youthspecialties.com/store
or your local Christian bookstore

youth specialties

800-776-8008
youthspecialties.com

real help for real ministry
EVENTS. RESOURCES. INTERNET.

National Youth Workers Convention

NYWC

A place where you and other youth workers can come together, worship, learn, and play.

To register go to youthspecialties.com/NYWC or call 888.346.4179
Registration forms are available online.

This curriculum course (based on Youth For Christ's 3Story training) offers an interactive learning experience that equips students to live and practice the 3Story way of life—a biblically based, culturally relevant form of discipleship-evangelism. With eight 50-minute training sessions, this curriculum kit is an ideal resource for teaching students how to build deep, authentic relationships with Jesus and genuine, transparent relationships with their friends.

3Story® Evangelism Training DVD Curriculum Kit
Preparing Teenagers for a Lifestyle of Evangelism
Youth for Christ
RETAIL $99.99
ISBN 0-310-27370-6

visit www.youthspecialties.com/store
or your local Christian bookstore

youth specialties